THE FLORIDA CAMPAIGN, 1774–83

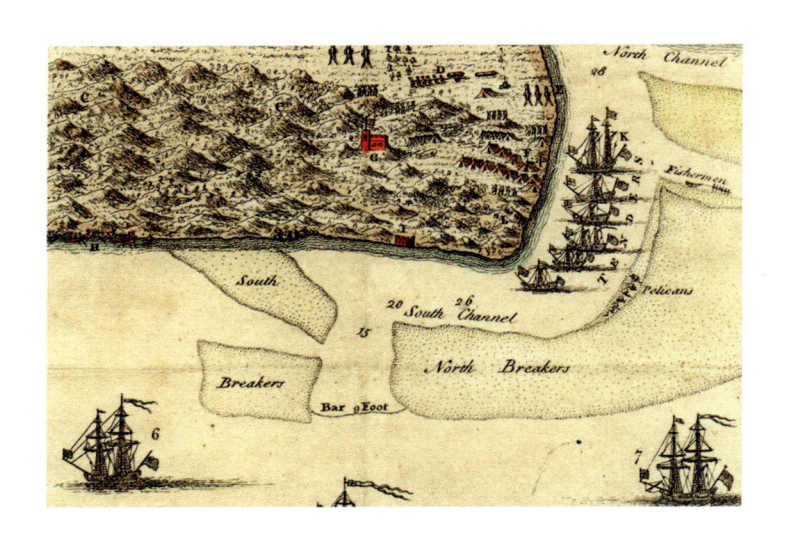

CASEMATE | ILLUSTRATED

THE FLORIDA CAMPAIGN, 1774–83

Robert Buccellato and Kartik Krishnaiyer

CIS0059

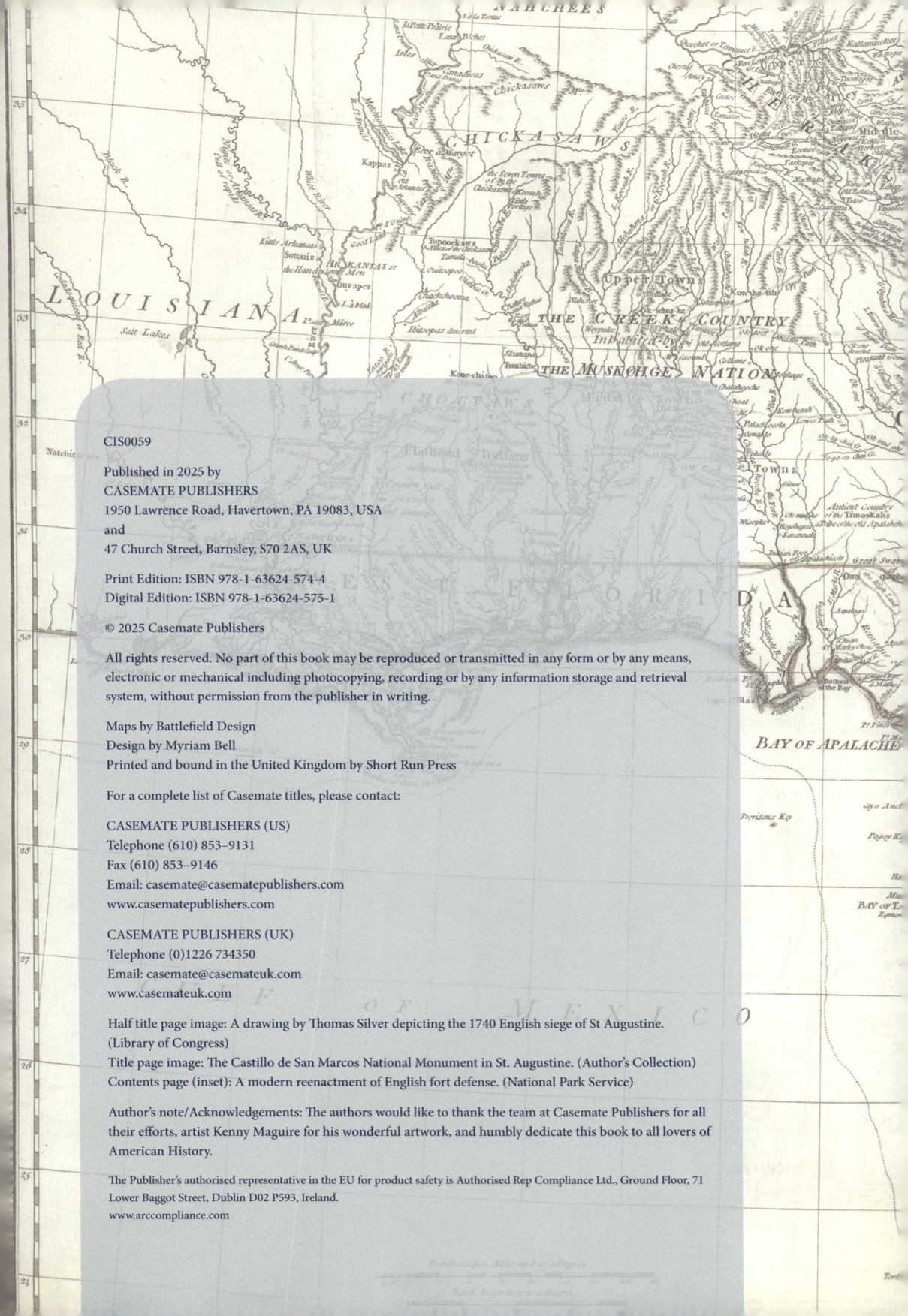

Published in 2025 by
CASEMATE PUBLISHERS
1950 Lawrence Road, Havertown, PA 19083, USA
and
47 Church Street, Barnsley, S70 2AS, UK

Print Edition: ISBN 978-1-63624-574-4
Digital Edition: ISBN 978-1-63624-575-1

© 2025 Casemate Publishers

All rights reserved. No part of this book may be reproduced or transmitted in any form or by any means, electronic or mechanical including photocopying, recording or by any information storage and retrieval system, without permission from the publisher in writing.

Maps by Battlefield Design
Design by Myriam Bell
Printed and bound in the United Kingdom by Short Run Press

For a complete list of Casemate titles, please contact:

CASEMATE PUBLISHERS (US)
Telephone (610) 853–9131
Fax (610) 853–9146
Email: casemate@casematepublishers.com
www.casematepublishers.com

CASEMATE PUBLISHERS (UK)
Telephone (0)1226 734350
Email: casemate@casemateuk.com
www.casemateuk.com

Half title page image: A drawing by Thomas Silver depicting the 1740 English siege of St Augustine. (Library of Congress)
Title page image: The Castillo de San Marcos National Monument in St. Augustine. (Author's Collection)
Contents page (inset): A modern reenactment of English fort defense. (National Park Service)

Author's note/Acknowledgements: The authors would like to thank the team at Casemate Publishers for all their efforts, artist Kenny Maguire for his wonderful artwork, and humbly dedicate this book to all lovers of American History.

The Publisher's authorised representative in the EU for product safety is Authorised Rep Compliance Ltd., Ground Floor, 71 Lower Baggot Street, Dublin D02 P593, Ireland.
www.arccompliance.com

Contents

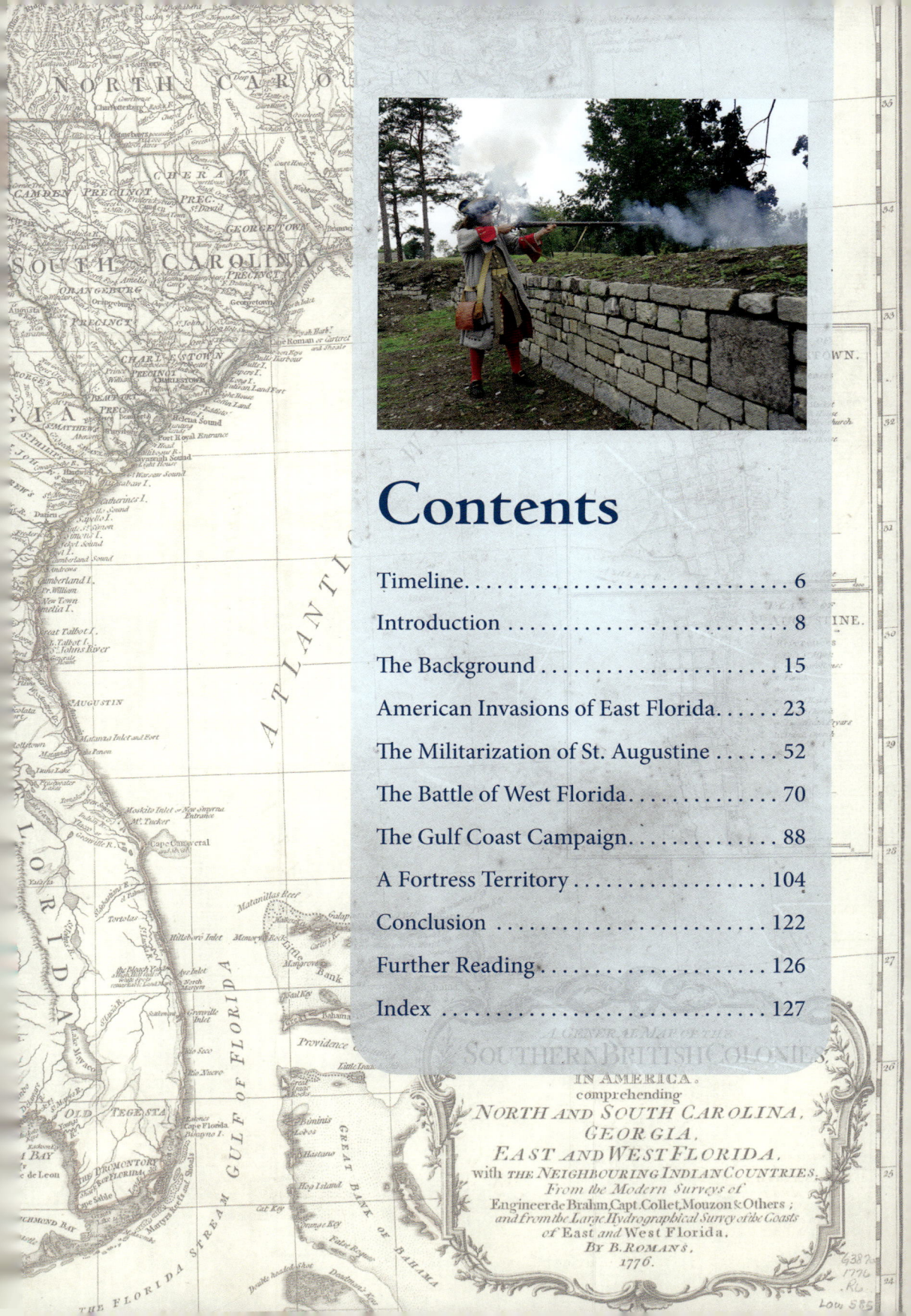

Timeline 6

Introduction 8

The Background 15

American Invasions of East Florida 23

The Militarization of St. Augustine 52

The Battle of West Florida 70

The Gulf Coast Campaign 88

A Fortress Territory 104

Conclusion 122

Further Reading 126

Index 127

Timeline

The Spanish Empire surrendered large sections of its North American holdings to the British Empire at the end of the Seven Years' War in 1763. The militarization of St. Augustine took place from that time until the return of Florida to the Spanish after the American Revolution. All events that took place between those two parallel moments in our story are presented below.

1763 — Florida is ceded to Great Britain.

1764 — Florida is split into East and West Florida along the Apalachicola River. Parts of West Florida west of the Perdido River were previously part of French Louisiana and part of the French cession to Britain at the end of the French and Indian (Seven Years') War.

1767 — New Smyrna Colony is founded south of St. Augustine.

▼ The cannons of Fort George in today's Pensacola. (National Park Service)

Timeline

1774	Patrick Tonyn becomes royal governor of East Florida.
1775	American Revolution begins; Whig (Patriot) government takes control of Georgia.
1776	First American invasion of East Florida.
1777	Second American invasion of East Florida; battle of Thomas Creek.
1778	Third American invasion of East Florida; battle of Alligator Creek Bridge.
1779	Spain enters the war on the American side; West Florida campaign begins.
1780	Charleston falls to the British; American prisoners are sent to St. Augustine.
1781	Spanish capture Pensacola; British surrender at Yorktown leads to exodus of Loyalists from the South to East Florida.
1782	East Florida population swells as Loyalists move into colony.
1783	British win naval battle off Florida coast; East Florida is ceded to Spain effective in 1784.
1784	Evacuation of East Florida is undertaken, and Spain takes control of the colony.

▼ Spanish coat of arms at Castillo de San Marcos. (National Park Service)
▼ ▶ The ruins of Fort Matanzas before its modern restoration. (Library of Congress)

Introduction

As young children in school, many of us learn about the American Revolution and the struggle of the original Thirteen Colonies for independence. We learn about how plucky, freedom-seeking Patriots fought the world's greatest power and prevailed. We learn about the ruthlessness of the British response. We learn about the supposed idealism and enlightenment that fueled the American rebel cause. History, however, tends to be written differently from generation to generation. Now, in the 21st century, historians are recognizing that by 1775, cracks were already showing in the edifice of Britain as the preeminent European power—surely still stronger than the others but increasingly dependent on foreign mercenaries and naval power. We also now recognize that the misplaced desire of the Bourbon kings in France and Spain to reclaim lost territory or prestige played a major role in the American victory.

▼ Typical living quarters of a British fort. (National Park Service)

▲ Fort Matanzas as it appears today. (Author's Collection)

Whatever the motivations for the Revolution and the incentives of both sides, Florida's important role in each of the above topics seems to be largely glossed over by those writing general histories of the era. This is especially true about Spain's pivotal role in using West Florida as a front in the war to squeeze the British, undoing the Crown's military strategy. We learn virtually nothing of St. Augustine's strategic importance and the repeated efforts of the Continental Army to capture it by invading East Florida.

East and West Florida declined to attend the first Continental Congress in the fall of 1774, despite being invited. The two Floridas were a hotbed of loyalism, with the likes of radicals Sam Adams, Joseph Warren, and John Hancock even being hung in effigy in St. Augustine.

During the war the colony of East Florida was led by Governor Patrick Tonyn, a prickly individual with a military background and autocratic manner.

Governor Tonyn was a staunch Loyalist, but as we will see throughout this work, as a conservative plantation owner and slave holder, he often clashed with other Loyalists and was more guarded about arming Africans and Native Americans than many of the other leaders around him. Nonetheless, he eventually was forced to give in on both counts as a war measure.

East Florida served as a major base for Loyalist and British operations throughout the war. As a staging ground for battle in the Southern Colonies, St. Augustine became critical to Britain's war plans. For this reason, it also became a target of American planning. This being the case does not mean the Patriot cause did not have sympathizers in East Florida. But on the whole, the majority of the population supported the British, and as the population swelled with Loyalists and runaway enslaved African people fleeing from colonies to the North, those with Patriot sympathies became badly outnumbered.

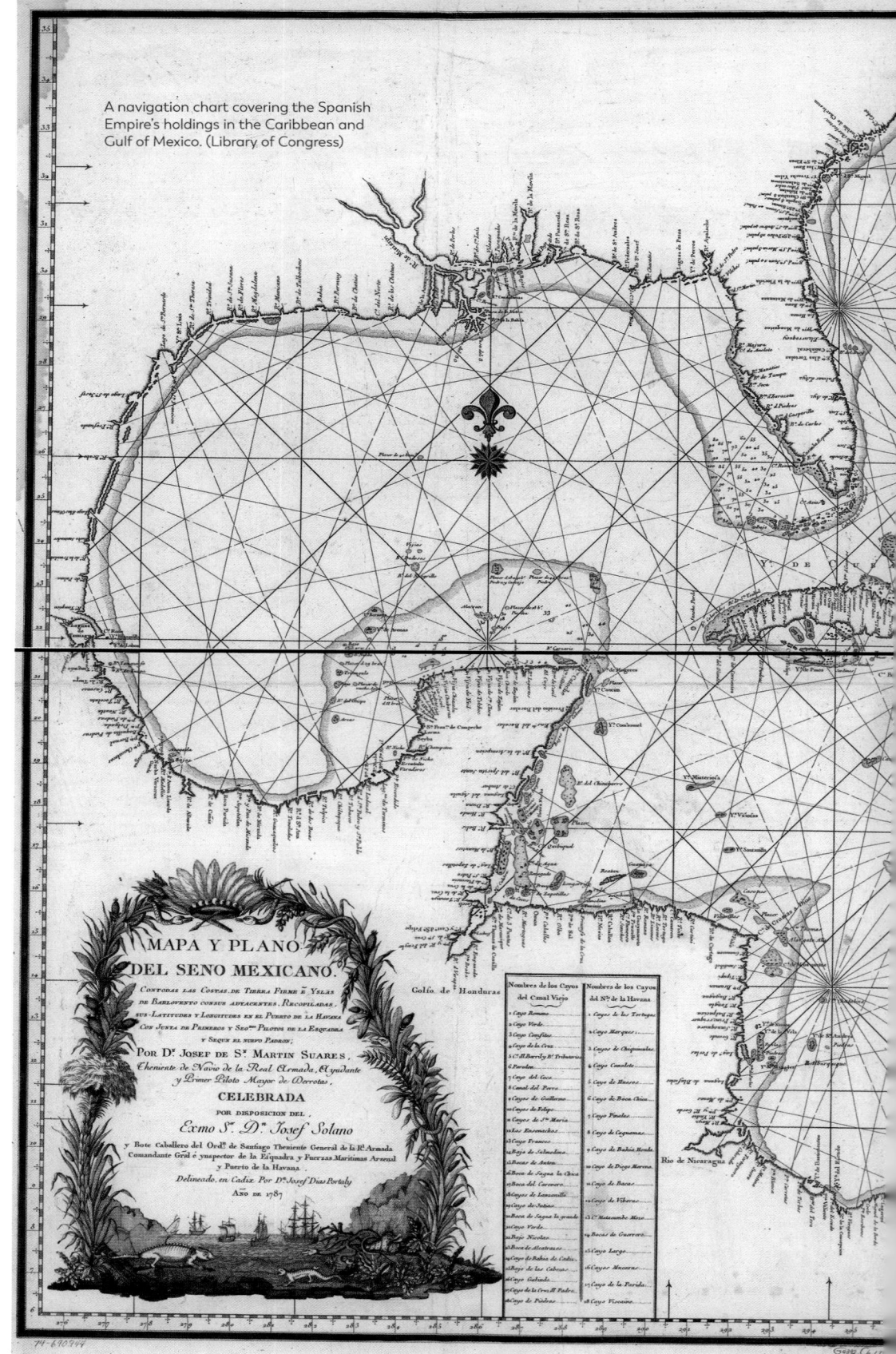

A navigation chart covering the Spanish Empire's holdings in the Caribbean and Gulf of Mexico. (Library of Congress)

MAPA Y PLANO DEL SENO MEXICANO.

CON TODAS LAS COSTAS DE TIERRA FIRME E YSLAS DE BARLOVENTO CON SUS ADYACENTES, RECOPILADAS, SUS LATITUDES Y LONGITUDES EN EL PUERTO DE LA HAVANA CON JUNTA DE PRIMEROS Y SEG.ᵒˢ PILOTOS DE LA ESQUADRA Y SEGUN EL NUEVO PADRON;

POR D.ⁿ JOSEF DE S.ᵗ MARTIN SUARES,
Theniente de Navio de la Real Armada, Ayudante
y Primer Piloto Mayor de Derrotas.

CELEBRADA

POR DISPOSICION DEL

Exmo S.ᵒʳ D.ⁿ Josef Solano

y Bote Caballero del Ord.ⁿ de Santiago Theniente General de la R.ᵃˡ Armada
Comandante Gral é ynspector de la Esquadra y Fuerzas Maritimas Arsenal
y Puerto de la Havana.

Delineado, en Cadiz Por D.ⁿ Josef Dias Portaly
AÑO de 1787.

Nombres de los Cayos del Canal Viejo	Nombres de los Cayos del N.ᵗᵉ de la Havana
1 Cayo Romano	1 Cayos de las Tortugas
2 Cayo Verde	2 Cayo Marques
3 Cayo Confites	3 Cayos de Chiquimulas
4 Cayo de la Cruz	4 Cayo Canaleto
5 C.ᵒ d.ˡ Borril y B.ᵒ Tributarios	
6 Paredon	
7 Cayo del Coco	5 Cayo de Huesos
8 Canal del Puerco	6 Cayo de Boca Chica
9 Cayos de Guillermo	7 Cayos Pinales
10 Cayos de Felipe	
11 Cayos de S.ᵗᵃ Maria	8 Cayo de Caguamas
12 Las Ensenachas	
13 Cayos Francos	9 Cayos de Bahia Honda
14 Baja de Almedina	
15 Bocas de Anton	10 Cayo de Diego Morena
16 Baja de Sagua la Chica	
17 Boca del Carenero	11 Cayo de Bacas
18 Cayos de Lanzanilla	
19 Cayo de Sotano	12 Cayo de Viboras
20 Boca de Sagua la grande	13 P.ᵗᵃ Matacumbe Moso
21 Cayo Verde	
22 Bajo Nicolas	14 Bocas de Guerrero
23 Boca de Alcatrases	
24 Cayos de Bahia de Cadiz	15 Cayo Largo
25 Bajo de las Cabezas	
26 Cayo Galindo	16 Cayos Mazarua
27 Cayo de la Cruz d.ˡ Padre	17 Cayo de la Parida
28 Cayo de Piedras	18 Cayo Vicaino

Golfo de Honduras

Rio de Nicaragua

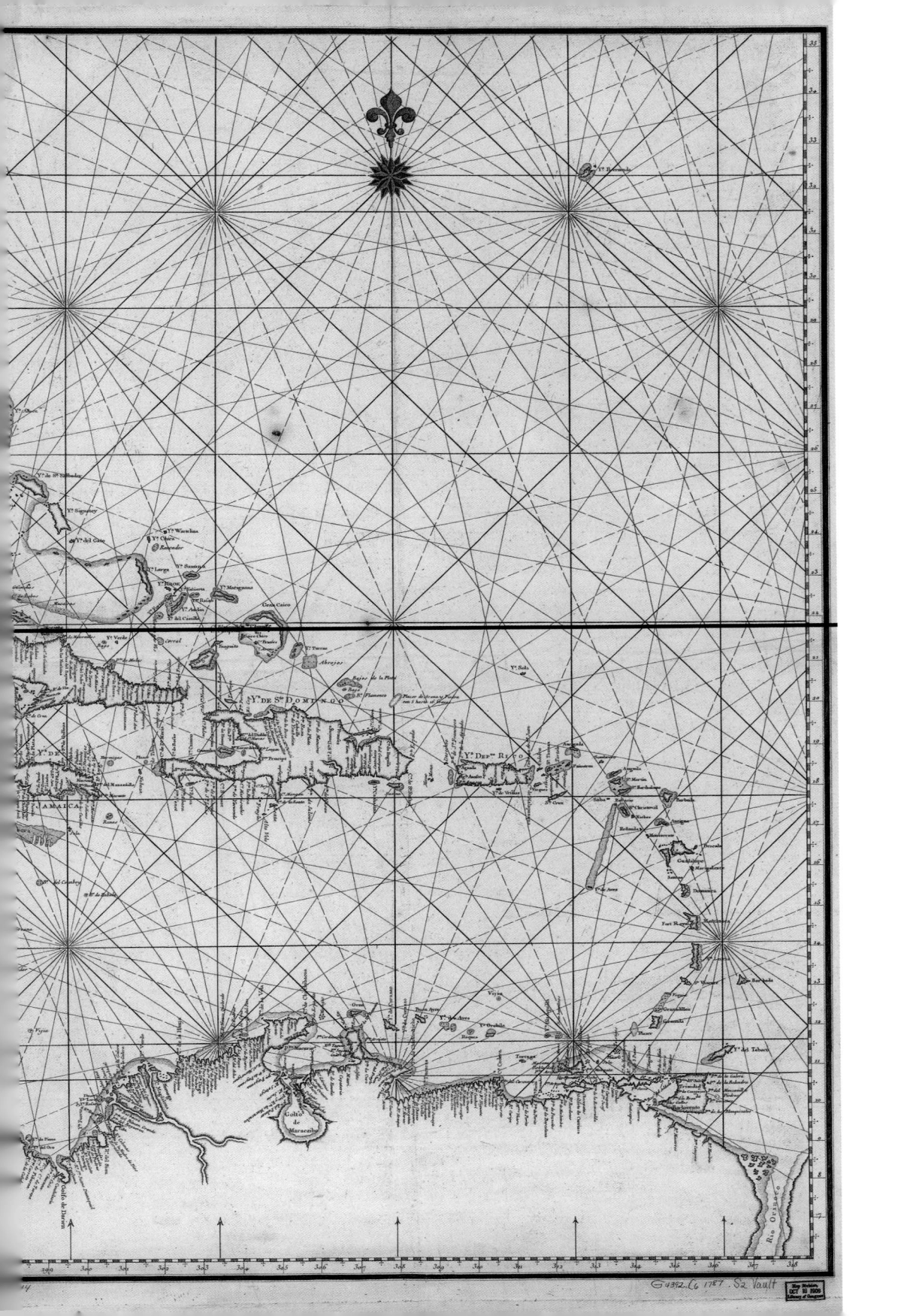

The Florida Campaign, 1774–83

▲ An early map of the Florida peninsula. (Florida State Archives)

During the Revolution the colony once again became a sanctuary for the runaway enslaved, much as it had been under Spanish rule in the period from 1693 to 1763. This at first made Governor Tonyn uncomfortable, and the colony became an odd mix, with many enslaved African people walking the same streets as free Black people who were eventually armed.

West Florida became a key objective in the war after Spain allied with the United States in 1779. The colorful exploits of the Spanish Governor of Louisiana General Bernardo de Gálvez, who liberated most of West Florida from British rule between 1779 and 1781, effectively crushing British hopes of holding Georgia, South Carolina, and East Florida, played a huge role in the general trajectory of the war. General Gálvez is a key figure in the history of North America who has faded into a certain degree of obscurity. In this work we will aim to bring him back to life.

As we will also discuss, the British intended East Florida to be a fortress colony. They did not intend to cede it in any peace settlement, but as we will see, they ended up handing the colony back to Spain in the treaties that followed the war, an act which created a hasty and

▶ A turret of present-day Fort Charlotte near Mobile, Alabama. (National Park Service)

unfortunate evacuation of what was a thriving colony at the time.

To present any volume on the history of the state of Florida and its place within the narrative of the American Revolutionary War can be as challenging and complex as charting the great expanse of the world's oceans. This state has grasped the imaginations of countless individuals for centuries and has played a role in every generation of colonial exploration. The conflict itself has taken on mythical qualities and still manages to inspire the imaginations of schoolchildren, writers, and history devotees to this day.

The purpose of this book is by no means to provide a definitive account of these events. Instead it provides an overdue focus on one major aspect of the historic upending of people and nations that was the American Revolutionary War. The images, maps, and artworks presented in this book will hopefully add a deeper dimension to these long-neglected events and personalities—transporting the reader to a time when the British empire was at the very summit of its power, the American Colonies were about to take center stage in one of the largest land transfers in human history, and a small part of the world known as British Florida was trapped in the middle.

▲ The Spanish territorial boundaries after the Seven Years' War. (Library of Congress)

The Background

The British assumed control of Florida in 1763 thanks to the Treaty of Paris. During the Seven Years' War, Britain had captured Havana and Spain traded Florida, which Britain saw as more strategically critical, back to the British for Havana.

▼ *The Piazza at Havana*, by Dominic Serres. British troops occupied Havana until 1763 and then returned it to Spain in exchange for Florida. (Library of Congress)

At the same time, French Louisiana was split, with the areas west of the Mississippi River given to Spain and the areas to the east given to Britain. Those eastern locales, which included Baton Rouge, Mobile, and Natchez, were added to Florida, and when the colony was divided between East and West Florida, they were governed from Pensacola.

For much of the colonial period, Britain ruled the seas, including the areas directly to Florida's north and east. Command of the seas made peninsular Florida, and its most important settlement, St. Augustine, a locale under constant pressure from the English. The Royal Navy and British-aligned pirate ships ruled the waters off the coast of Florida for a large portion of Florida's first Spanish period.

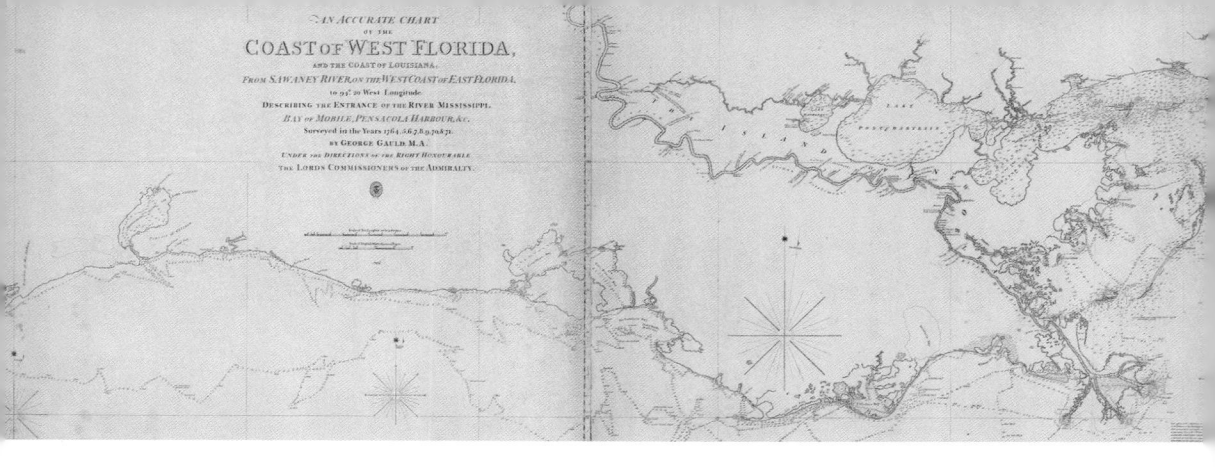

Florida was prosperous in the 1600s, probably more economically advanced and self-sufficient than the English colonies to the north. However, the 1670 founding of Charles Town (now Charleston) fundamentally reshaped Spanish Florida and would ultimately result in St. Augustine becoming more militarized and the

▲ A chart of the coastline of West Florida. (Library of Congress)

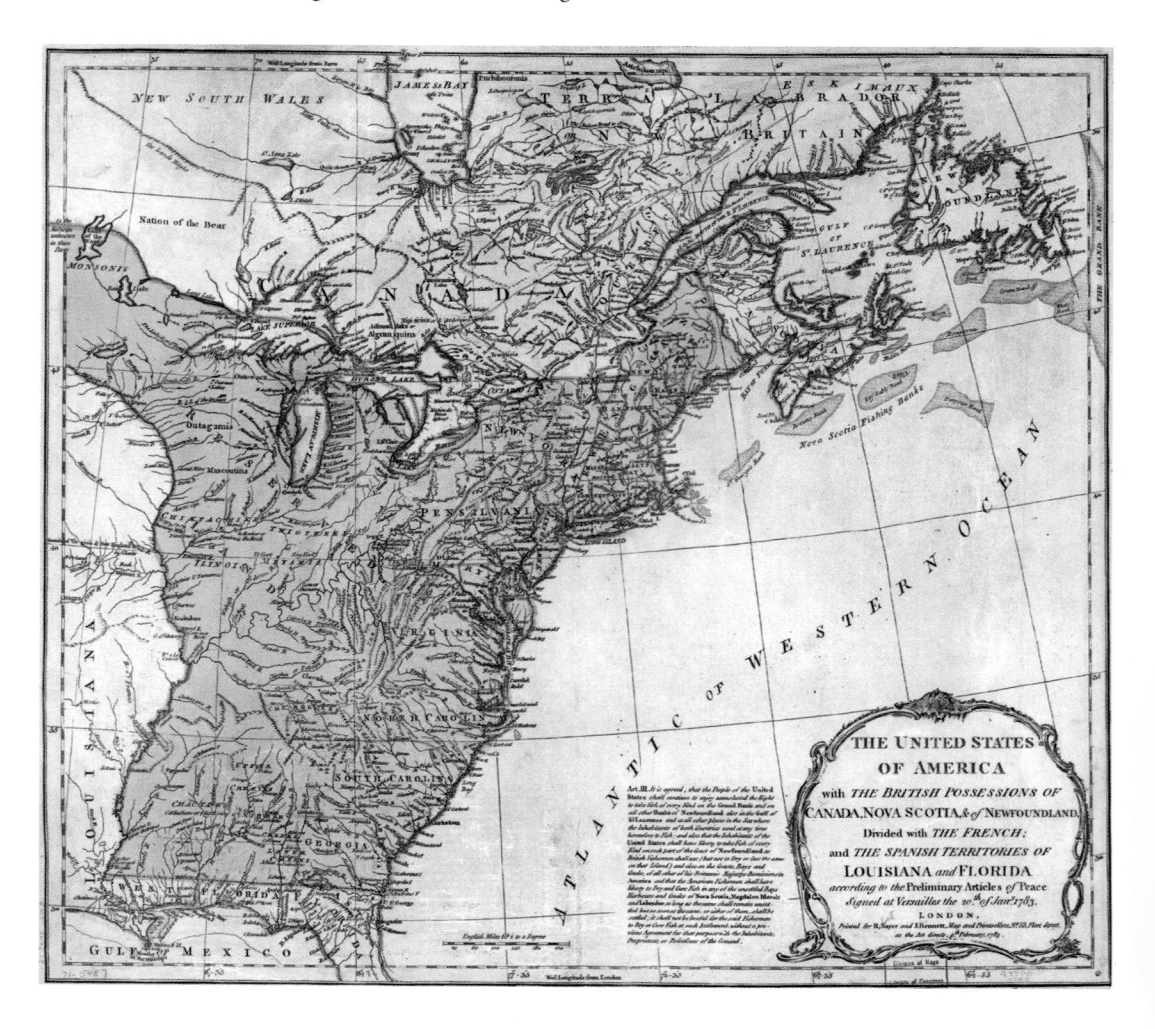

Profile:
Governor Patrick Tonyn (1725–1804)

▶ British General Patrick Tonyn, the last British governor of East Florida. (Library of Congress)

◀ A map of the United States of America, Canada, Nova Scotia, Newfoundland, Louisiana, and Florida in 1783. (Library of Congress)

Patrick Tonyn served 10 years as the royal governor of East Florida (1774–84), during which he steered the colony toward being a Loyalist stronghold in the American Revolution. Despite personal qualms, Governor Tonyn is credited with raising regiments of formerly enslaved African people and arming them to fight on the British side. He also enabled the formation of the East Florida Rangers which became a nimble and effective fighting unit.

Tonyn's leadership, though, was questioned throughout the war. For example, in August 1775, the British vessel *Brig* bound for St. Augustine to reinforce the city was seized by Patriot forces. Its provisions were sent north. Tonyn had sent many of St. Augustine's provisions to Boston earlier in the year. Now, residents were effectively without protection from a potential Patriot attack.

Tonyn's leadership style was considered prickly by many of the leading citizens of the colony. He regularly clashed with leading citizens like John Stuart, settlers like Andrew Turnbull, and just about every military commander assigned to the protection of the colony.

Nonetheless, he was able to keep East Florida out of rebel hands while molding a colony which sported free Africans, armed Native Americans, and white settlers, a rarity in British North America.

The Florida Campaign, 1774–83

The Background

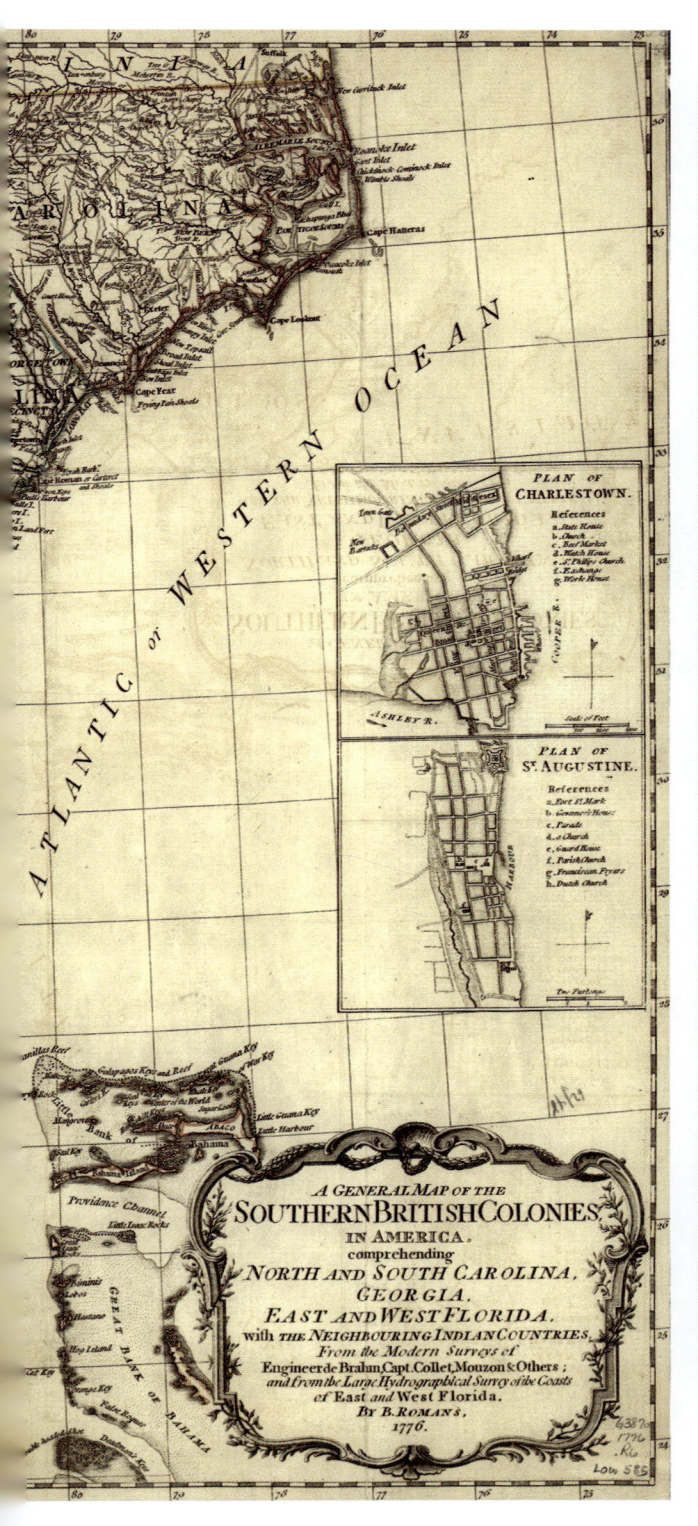

The Florida Citrus Industry

The British taste for exotic goods fueled the conquest of India and parts of the Caribbean. Beginning in the 1500s the English had formed various trading entities to procure exotic goods from Russia, the Ottoman Empire, and South Asia. Much like these exotic locations, East Florida provided another good that piqued curiosity for the elites back at home—oranges.

During the Spanish period a few groves in and around St. Augustine exported oranges regularly to British colonies farther north. But once Britain got its hands on Florida in 1763, increased orange production began, as did innovative techniques to preserve their quality for the long Atlantic journey. Florida's first citrus baron was an English merchant, Jesse Fish, who used land he owned on Anastasia Island to plant orange trees and export the fruit to the Thirteen Colonies as well as directly to London. Even after war broke out in 1775, this export trade continued as both the colonial and British tastes for oranges had exploded since 1763!

◀ The Southern theater of war in the Revolution. (Library of Congress)

The Florida Campaign, 1774–83

The Background

◀ The Stamp Act of 1765 was one of the leading causes of the conflict. (Library of Congress)

◀▼ Political propaganda was a large part of colonial life leading into the American Revolutionary War. (Library of Congress)

▼ The American Rattle Snake, a symbol of the Patriot rebellion. (Library of Congress)

economy of Florida spiraling downward. Florida's prosperity and geographic location made it a constant English target.

Queen Anne's War proved the end of Florida's golden period as a Spanish colony. During the war, the English invaded Florida in 1702, again in 1704, and finally in 1707. The Spanish held on to Florida, but the result was a far less prosperous colony than Spain had governed in the 1600s. Florida's population plunged, missions were abandoned, and the colony was militarized.

Spain now saw Florida more strategically as a bulwark against possible British expansion in the Caribbean. The English had captured Jamaica in 1655, leading to an era of unmatched piracy in the region. Florida was a regular target of these pirates, as was Cuba, a colony Spain deeply valued economically.

Another attempt to capture Florida was made by the British during the War of Jenkins' Ear. By this time, colonists in Britain's southernmost North American settlements had established a thriving plantation culture, and Spain's willingness to harbor the runaway enslaved in Florida had become a major problem for the British. In both 1740 and 1742 British expeditions attempted to capture St. Augustine and both times failed.

Britain's Divide and Conquer Strategy

British imperial policy first applied in North America, then tried in India during the conquest of Bengal from 1757 to 1765, and finally perfected in the post-1798 subjugation of Ireland, was on full display during the American Revolution.

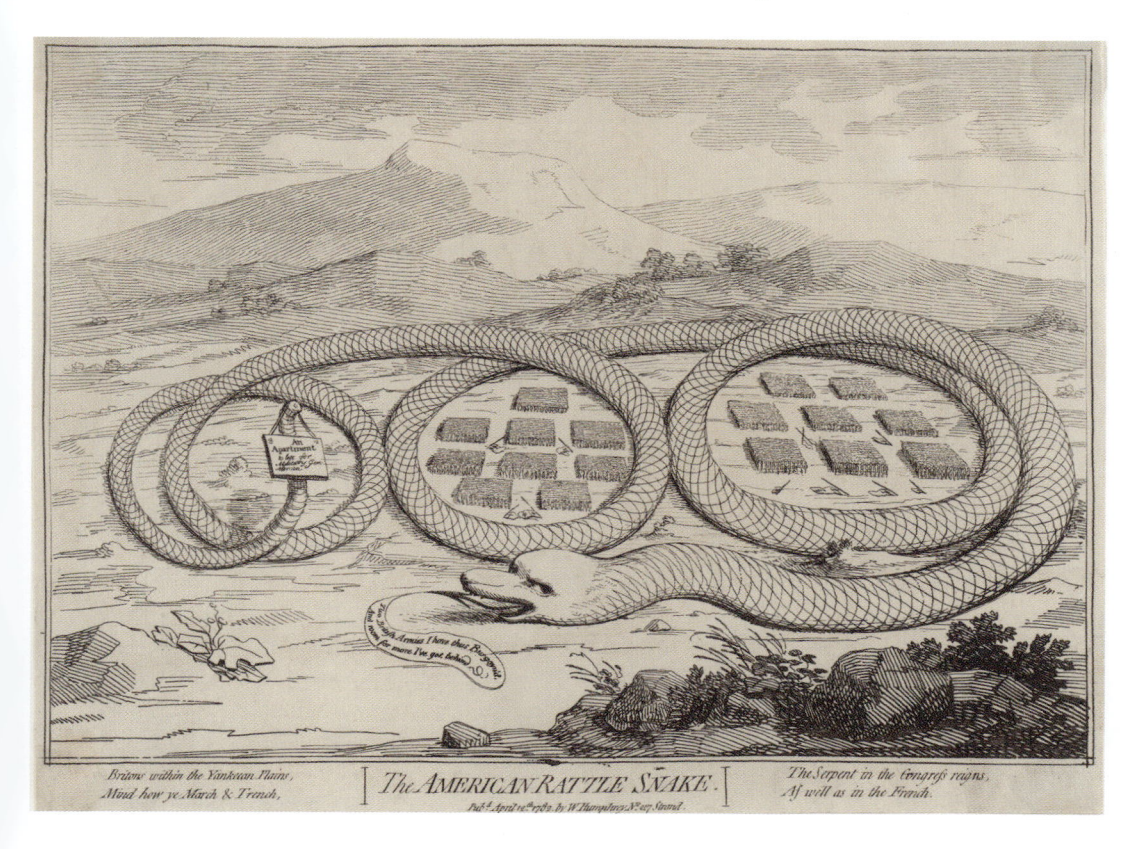

Britons within the Yankeean Plains, Mind how ye March & Trench. | The AMERICAN RATTLE SNAKE. | *The Serpent in the Congress reigns, As well as in the French.*

The British would seek to divide those in the colonies by religion, ethnicity, race, or any other means. British officials who at one time were anti-Catholic and violently racist, suddenly became agnostic when it came to these issues, and during the Revolutionary period cultivated Catholic, African American, and Native American allies.

This speaks to a lack of ideology within the British ranks. However, empire and commercial considerations were always at the forefront of why decisions were made. The British would use whatever means and cultivate disparate allies to achieve their commercial and imperial goals.

Florida's Role in Trade with Britain and the West Indies

The United Colonies had made economic warfare an essential part of their arsenal. Since East and West Florida were almost entirely dependent for prosperity on trade and subsidies from Britain, this economic war would disproportionately target Florida. The boycott of British goods and the lack of capital flowing from the colonies rebelling against the Crown, in turn, had a negative impact on Florida.

In British eyes, Florida was part of both the Caribbean and North America. This led to a strategy which made Florida a beachhead to protect British possessions both to the north and among the islands to the south. It is often forgotten that during this era of history, Britain's West Indian possessions were more critical to the Crown than North America.

The reality is that very little commerce took place between Florida and the colonies to the north. There was almost no connection to New England, Pennsylvania, or New York, and the connections to the southernmost colonies were based around transplants who tended to be more loyal to the Crown than those who remained in Georgia and the Carolinas.

If anything, the boycott of British goods by the colonies to the north pushed Florida's residents closer to the Crown.

Much of Florida's population was new to the region and had no historic ties to democratic institutions. While democratic philosophies and inclinations had flourished in British North America, they were largely absent in New Spain.

Unlike the Thirteen Colonies, Florida had never had the sort of experience with town halls and local councils that the British emigrants to the North had. Most recent migrants to Florida had come from places such as Minorca or the Ottoman Empire where democracy did not exist.

During the course of the war, as we will dive into later, East Florida elected a colonial legislature but West Florida never did.

▲ Reminders of Spanish rule were everywhere in British Florida. (Library of Congress)

American Invasions of East Florida

During the Revolution the American rebels made several failed attempts to invade East Florida and ultimately capture St. Augustine. In addition to these direct invasions, raiding was a very common occurrence along the Georgia–East Florida border just north and south of the St. Marys River. While this is a long-neglected front in popular lore, fighting in one form or another lasted for almost the entire duration of the conflict.

▼ *Border Skirmishes*, a painting by Sidney E. King. (National Park Service)

The Florida Campaign, 1774–83

Much of the war in East Florida was based around the border between Florida and Georgia. From the foundation of Georgia in 1733 until Florida became a U.S. Territory in 1821, this border was constantly either in dispute or the scene of potential trouble. During this period, only between 1763 and 1775 were Florida and Georgia flying under the same flag.

To understand the dynamics of this conflict we need to briefly cover earlier 18th-century history. Georgia was

▼ A map of the Province of Georgia, created in the late 1770s. (Library of Congress)

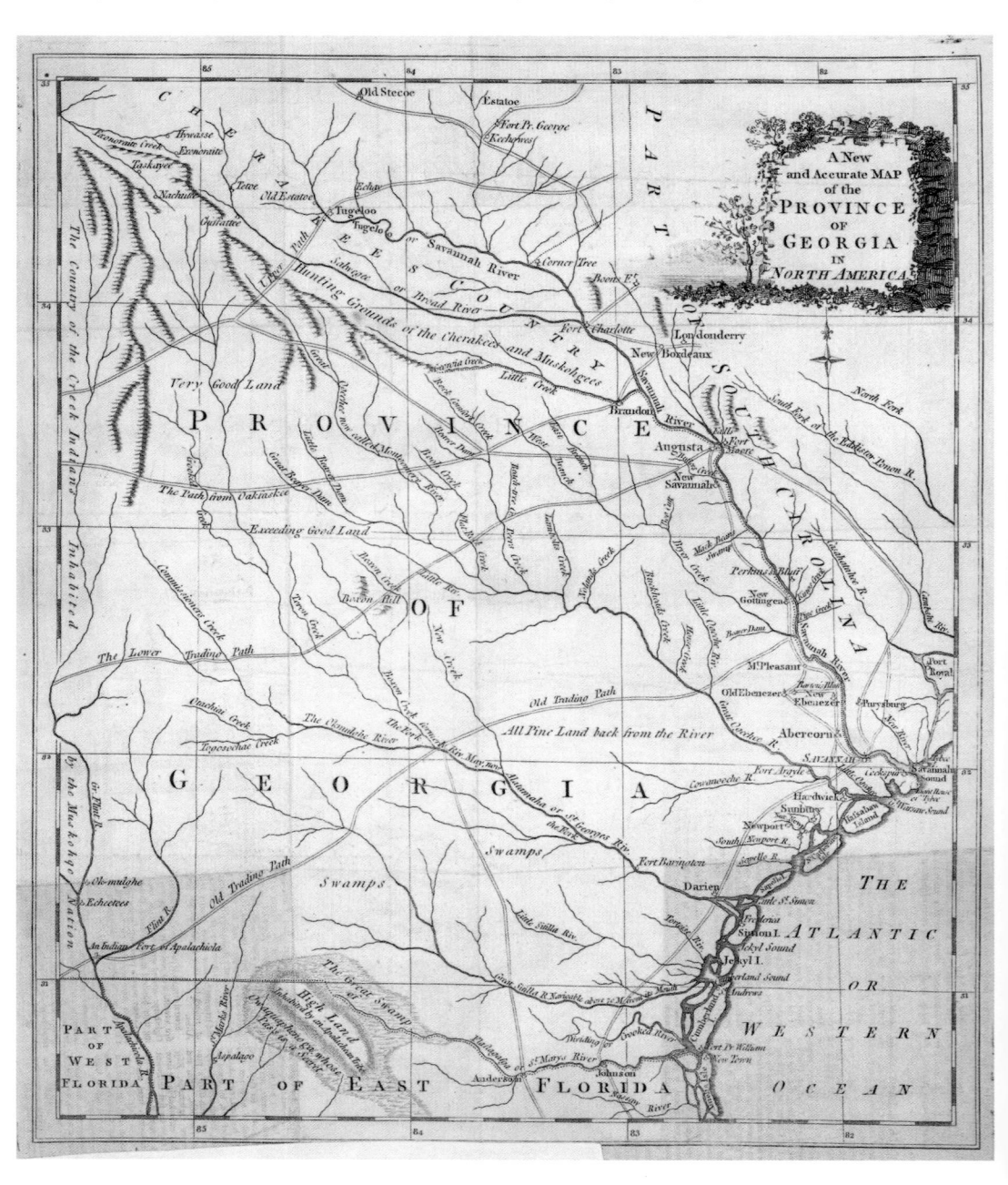

founded by James Oglethorpe in 1733 as a penal colony, but also as a buffer area for the British against Spanish Florida. Florida under the Spanish had been a haven for the runaway enslaved, and St. Augustine had by this time become a heavily fortified town that posed a threat to British holdings in the region.

Between Georgia's founding in 1733 and Florida's cession to the United States in 1819, armed conflicts regularly took place near or along the border. In fact, the battles

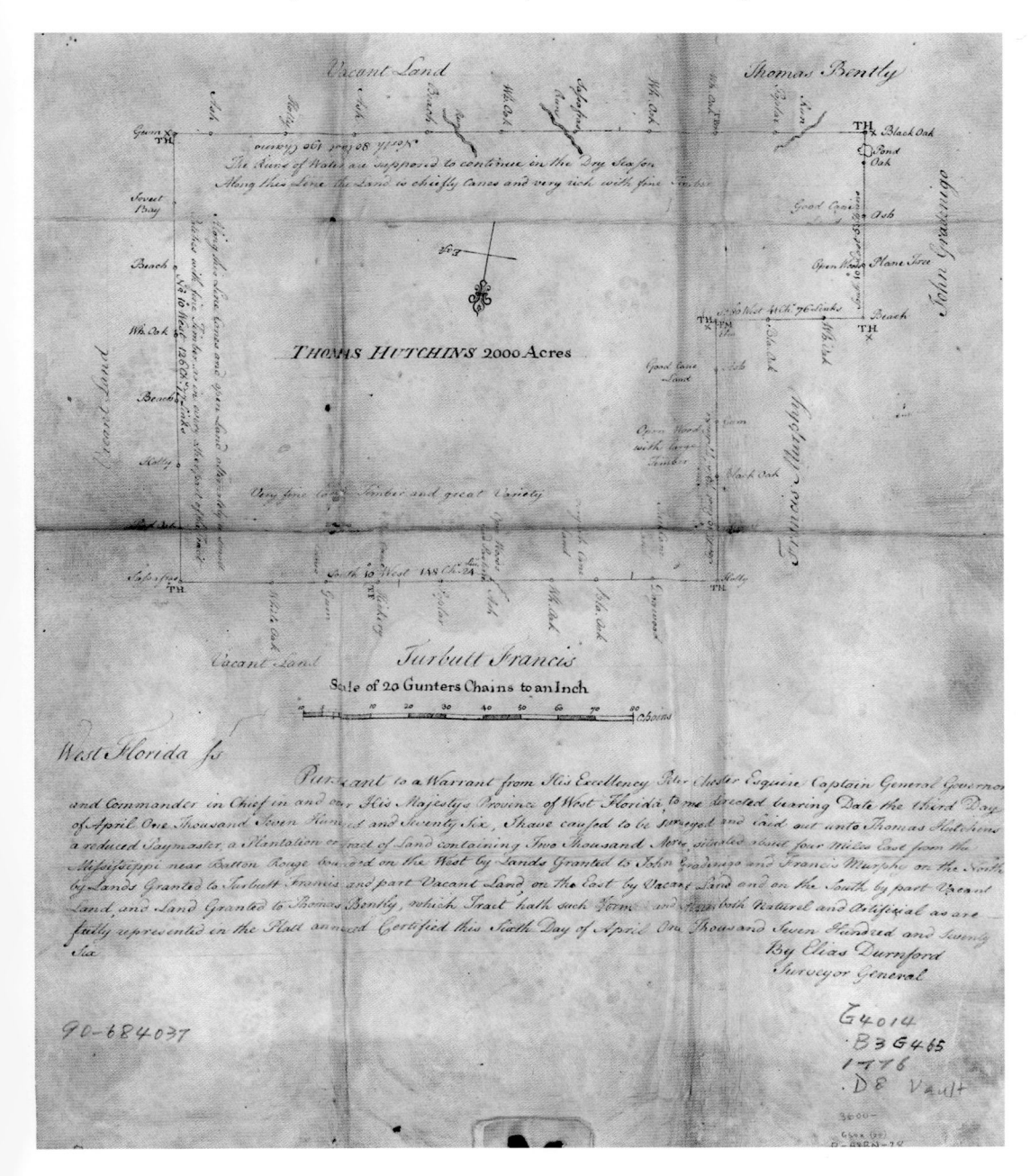

▼ A land grant issued to British subjects. (Florida State Archives)

The Florida Campaign, 1774–83

◄ Various Native American tribes fought on all sides of this conflict. (Artist Kenny Maguire)

◄ Colonial troops preparing to march into Florida. (Library of Congress)

that sprung up were a semi-regular event, in 1740–42, 1775–81, 1795, and 1812–13, plus several smaller skirmishes along the way.

When the British initially founded Georgia as a strategic hedge against Spanish Florida it was to be a whites-only colony. This was done to mitigate the threat of runaway slaves from other colonies escaping to Florida. In fact, historian Gerald Horne has called Georgia the key to the construction of a "white pro-slavery wall" as a bulwark against St. Augustine.

The willingness of Spanish officials to aid in harboring and eventually arming runaway slaves made St. Augustine a constant target of white settlers to the North. The British colonists residing from Georgia to Virginia along the Atlantic Seaboard could not feel safe until St. Augustine was flying under the same flag they were.

So while much of the written history of the United States has recorded Georgia being founded as a penal colony, the ultimate motivation for its creation was without question Florida's growing militarization and the Spanish colony's increasing role as a haven for runaway slaves. A penal colony could have, and probably would have, been founded elsewhere if not for the presence of Florida to the south and the need for the British to create a bulwark as a result. Spain had claimed territory well to the north of the St. Marys River as part of Florida, and it would not relinquish these claims until 1750, which came eight years after an invading force from Florida was defeated at Fort Frederica on St. Simons Island.

When the British assumed control of Florida in 1763, efforts were made to establish a plantation-based economy much like its neighbors to the north. While Florida did develop some large plantations, its topography and climate were inhospitable in much of the colony. In addition, the types of crops that would grow were different than in places like

The Florida Campaign, 1774–83

Virginia or South Carolina, though indigo cultivation, unlike in the sister colony of West Florida, was somewhat successful.

St. Augustine's population was augmented by many colonists from outside the British Isles who were imported to East Florida. This population was fundamentally different from that of the British colonies to the north, and with a domestic economy that wasn't fully mature, ties to the mother country and the trade network around the Caribbean were critical to East Florida's survival. But a uniformity never existed among the colonists, as we will explore.

After the battles of Lexington and Concord in April 1775, British Commander in Chief General Thomas Gage ordered 150 soldiers to leave St. Augustine and fortify Savannah, the capital of Georgia. However, the Loyalists were ousted in Georgia, and with the Whig (Patriot) takeover of the state, East Florida's soldiers returned home.

Following the Crown's loss of Georgia to the American rebels in 1775, conflict would once again spring up along the border.

General George Washington and the Continental Congress Decide to Move Against East Florida

In December 1775, Continental Army General George Washington was informed that the British had been stockpiling weaponry, ammunition, and other materials in St. Augustine. At this point General Washington began to prepare defensive actions in the event the British launched an invasion of the Southern Colonies from East Florida. Additional fortifications were ordered in Savannah, and other outposts were reinforced.

The concern was so great that within weeks the political leadership in

▼ Invasion of British East Florida historical marker. (Author's Collection)

▲ The blockhouse of Fort King George in McIntosh County, Georgia, reconstructed in 1988. (State of Georgia)

▼ Historical marker for Fort King George. (Author's Collection)

Philadelphia decided they would rather take offensive action against East Florida preemptively than wait for the seemingly inevitable British invasion.

In January 1776, the Continental Congress authorized the Southern Colonies to attack St. Augustine and capture it in order to safeguard the Patriot cause. The Congress resolved "that the seizing and securing the barracks and castle of St. Augustine will greatly contribute to the safety of the colonies." Additionally, capturing St. Augustine would give the Continental Army control of the town's guardian fortress, the Castillo de San Marcos, and thus the ability to directly resist any invading British Army coming from the West Indies. The fort had been successfully held as a Spanish outpost against British sieges in both 1702 and 1740.

A serious miscalculation was made in the Continental Congress, however, similar to the mistake made in the Quebec campaign. This was an assumption that the general population of East Florida would rise up if given the opportunity. St. Augustine by this time was filling up with Loyalists and runaway slaves, and also had many Crown-aligned Native Americans either in the town or nearby. After the collapse of the New Smyrna Colony, due to disease and

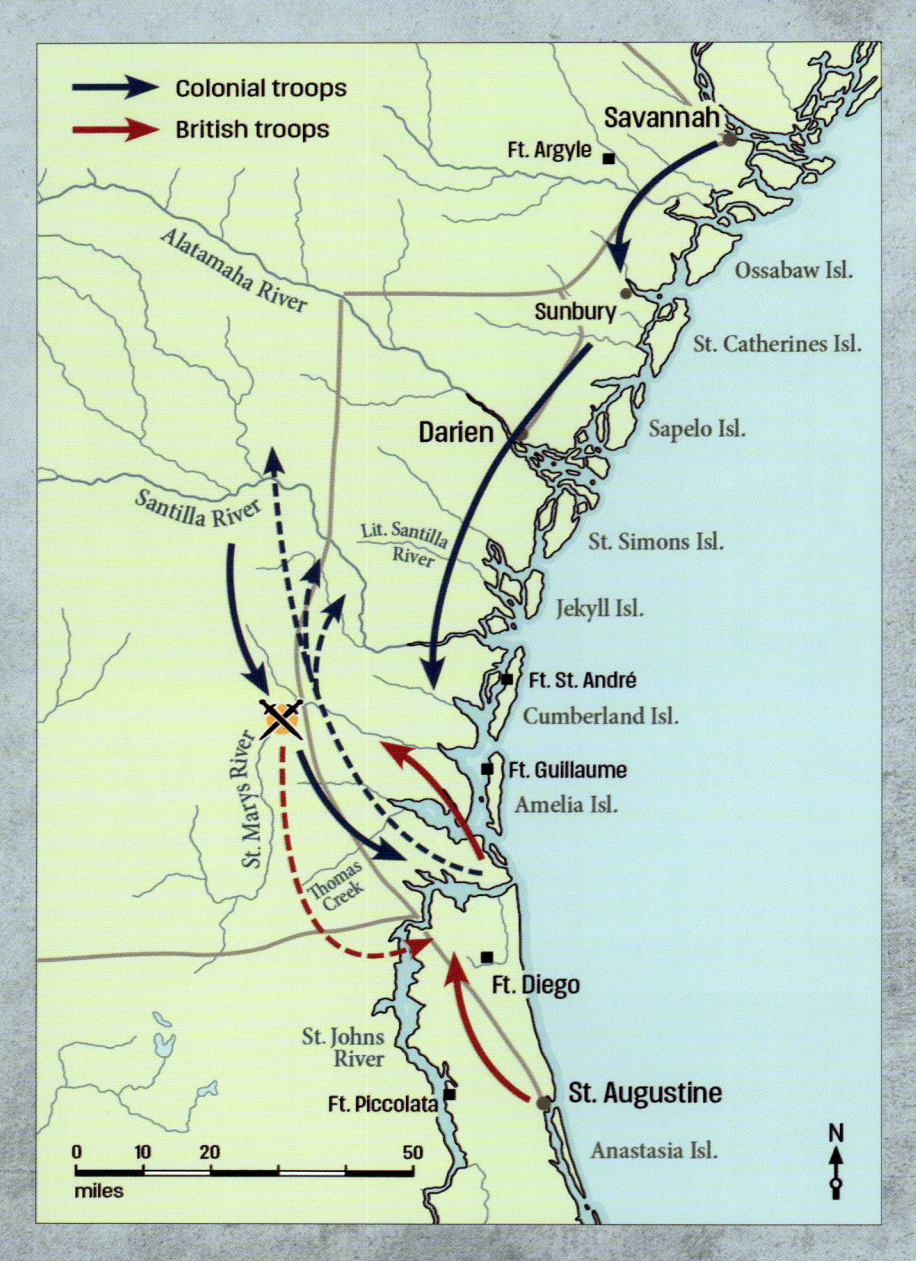

▲ Colonial and British troop movements around the Georgia–East Florida border in 1776 and 1777.

All three foreign superpowers competed for Florida's land. (Author's Collection)

brutal mismanagement, the area around St. Augustine represented the only major population center in East Florida. While New Smyrna, with its Minorcan and Greek Orthodox communities, might have been ripe for rebellion, once its people were absorbed into St. Augustine, they were a minority.

First Attempted American Invasion of East Florida

Invading East Florida from Georgia requires traversing miles and miles of cypress swamps and boggy lands crawling with alligators and mosquitos as well as crossing several creeks and streams that cut through swampy areas. The general region has remained so inhospitable it is still one of the least populated areas of both Florida and Georgia. These logistical hurdles would prove difficult to overcome, but beginning in 1776, the American Patriots tried time and again to cross this area to reach St. Augustine, which they saw as a vital objective in the war.

Continental Congress member Governor John Rutledge of South Carolina was sent south in early 1776 to oversee

Fort King George was constructed in the Savannah–Altamaha River region. (Author's Collection)

the conquest of St. Augustine and the formation of an American government in East Florida. He expected to learn of triumphant marches by Continental troops into the region.

However, Major General Charles Lee, who was the Continental Army's ranking commander in the South and assigned to mount an invasion of East Florida by General Washington, hadn't moved yet.

◄ Fort King George sentry post. (State of Georgia)

◄ The reconstructed outer walls of Fort King George. (State of Georgia)

▶ Fort King George cannons prepared to meet any opposing troops. (Library of Congress)

Major General Lee was an experienced British-born officer, and by 1776 had ascended to second in command behind General Washington. But Major General Lee dithered on the invasion, perhaps prudently but losing potentially valuable time.

In fact, British forces had anticipated the coming invasion as early as May 30, 1776, and had massed along the St Marys River which marked the boundary between Georgia and East Florida. In fact, had the British been more aggressive they could have moved into Southern Georgia with little resistance since the Patriots were not organized at the time. But the British were in a strictly defensive posture in the region.

Major General Lee was eventually recalled and sent to New York in November of 1776. As most Revolutionary War buffs know, Major General Lee coveted General Washington's command, became overtly critical of him, and eventually blundered

▶ Cannons positioned along the outer wall. (National Historic Park)

The Florida Campaign, 1774–83

into being captured by the British two weeks before General Washington's epic crossing of the Delaware.

But before Major General Lee's recall he was joined in Georgia by American General Robert Howe (no relation to the British brothers, general and admiral). In August 1776, Major General Lee and General Howe prepared for the invasion. The previous year the Continental Army under General Richard Montgomery had invaded British-held Quebec, but General Montgomery had been killed and Captain Benedict Arnold had been forced to lead a torturous retreat back into New York.

This would be the second foray of the Continental Army into British territory outside the original Thirteen Colonies, and it would prove just as disastrous.

Major General Lee's forces, numbering 2,500, were planning to march south from Savannah and eventually take boats to the coastal town of Darien, Georgia. Not enough boats were commissioned to transport all the troops, so many marched southwards. Food was scarce and the marching became insufferable for many troops. Large numbers of desertions took place, illness spread among the men, and the mission was eventually abandoned. A few troops made it to the border of East Florida along the Kings Road (built by the British in the 1760s) but by December 1776 could go no farther due to their lack of food and supplies.

The Continental Army had been losing 10 to 15 men a day while the Georgia militia penetrated deeper, almost to the St. Johns River, temporarily holding the territories between the St. Johns and St. Marys rivers

▼ A view from Fort King George's northeast sentry tower. (National Historic Park)

▲ How Fort King George must have appeared to an approaching enemy. (National Historic Park)

in East Florida. But raids back home in Georgia by British irregulars forced the militia to withdraw and the Continental Army contingent also retreated. The first invasion of Florida fizzled out. One benefit of the campaign for the Continental forces, however, was the construction of Fort Rowe and Fort McIntosh to protect the Kings Road, which ran from St. Augustine into Southern Georgia. These structures would prove helpful to the Patriot cause further along in the war.

Second Attempted American Invasion of East Florida

As the precursor to a renewed invasion, in March 1777 General Washington wrote to both General Howe and Georgia Council of Safety member Jonathan Bryan urging speedy military action against East Florida. But General Howe, seemingly burnt by the first invasion, plus the difficulty of coordinating with local militia, dallied too

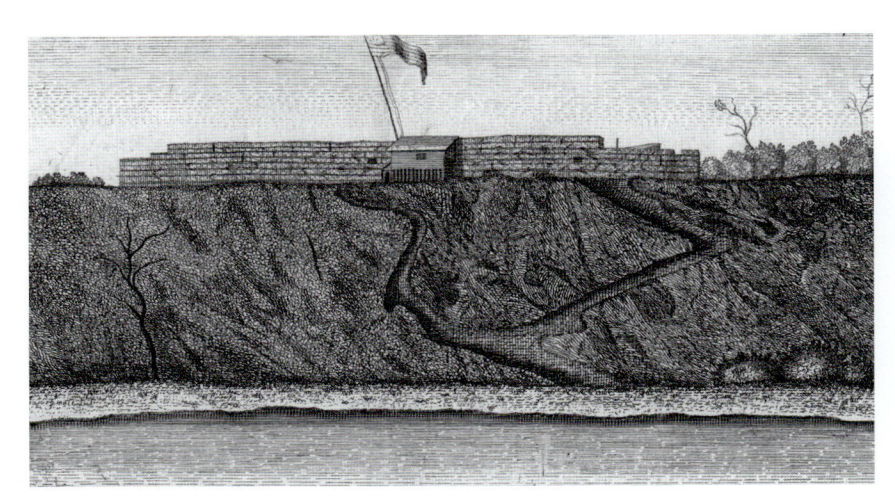

▶ An artist's rendering of Fort McIntosh. (Library of Congress)

35

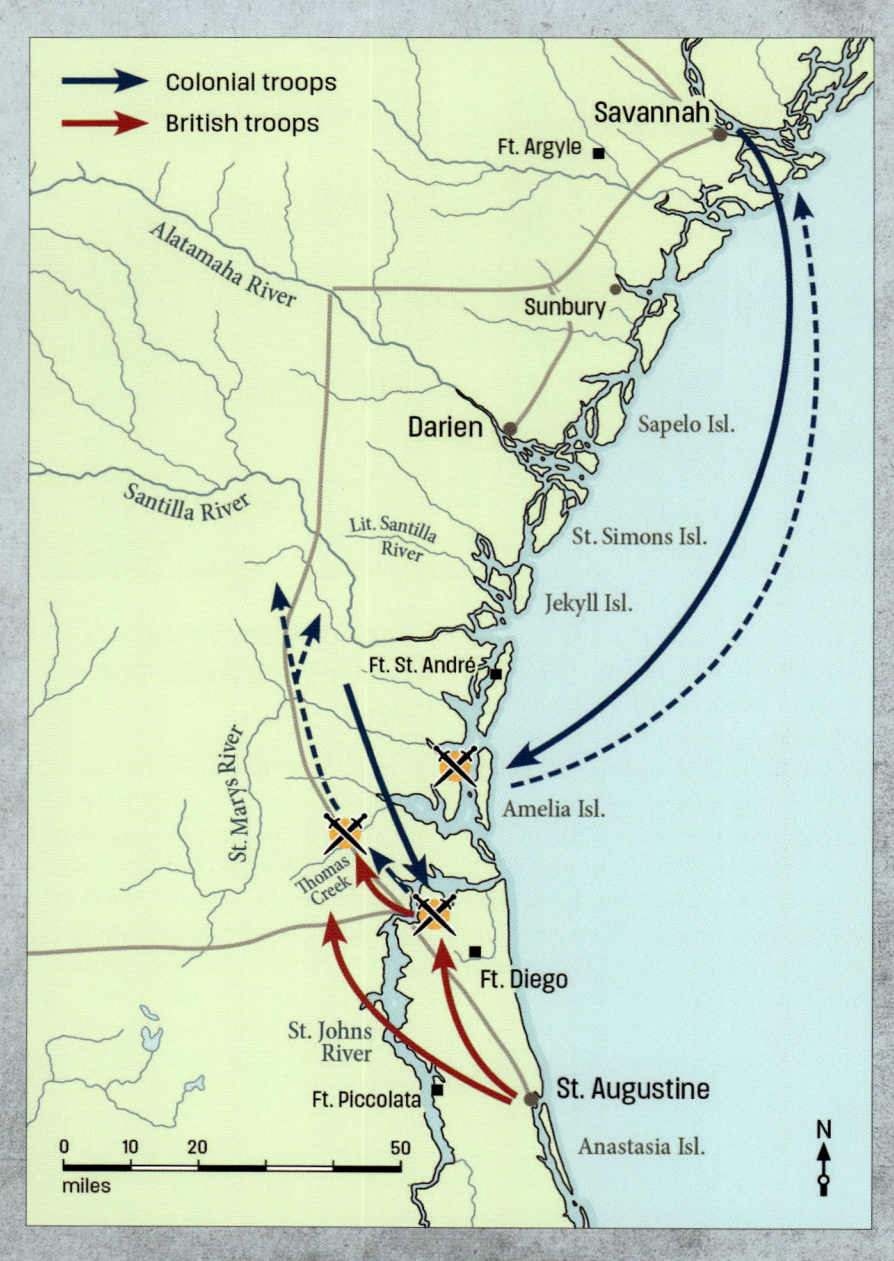

▲ Troop movements leading to the battle of Thomas Creek.

American Invasions of East Florida

long, and the offensive move against Florida fell to Georgia Governor Button Gwinnett.

At this point the British promoted Governor Tonyn to the rank of colonel, and with his new rank Governor Tonyn decided to aggressively pursue a strategy which fused together anybody willing to fight for the Crown regardless of race.

The East Florida Rangers

A new British militia force emerged to protect Florida in early 1777: the East Florida Rangers. This new creation was a direct result of Governor Tonyn's new rank, and he took advantage of fleeing Loyalists coming to East Florida as well as the large numbers of native allies that had been cultivated from the start of the war onward.

Lieutenant Colonel Thomas Brown, a Loyalist Georgia plantation owner, had been taken prisoner and tortured by the Sons of Liberty in 1775 soon after the Whig takeover of the colony. Brown suffered a fractured skull and lost two toes during the assaults, which included being tarred and feathered.

Instead of scaring Lieutenant Colonel Brown into submission, the rebels had created an enemy who would work to organize Loyalist and Native American resistance to the American cause for the duration of the war. And despite being a plantation owner who previously held African enslaved people, Lieutenant Colonel Brown would prove willing to arm Black people to fight against the Patriots later in the war.

Lieutenant Colonel Brown set up a network of Loyalist allies from East Florida to North Carolina, and spent a year living among the Native Americans, winning their trust and forming an alliance that persisted through the conflict. Lieutenant Colonel Brown, much like Governor Tonyn, found relations with the Native Americans easier to manage once it

▲ This was not the typical uniform for a colonial soldier. But French funding ensured that the American army could attain at least a veneer of professionalism. (Library of Congress)

Profile:
Lieutenant Colonel Thomas Brown (1750–1825)

Thomas Brown, a Loyalist Georgia plantation owner, refused to sign an oath swearing Loyalty to the Continental Congress. He was taken prisoner and tortured by the Sons of Liberty on August 2, 1775, soon after the Whig takeover of the colony. Brown suffered a fractured skull after he was hit with the butt of a rifle, and lost two toes from the actions, which included being tarred and feathered and tied to a tree.

By taking this action, the rebels had created an enemy who would work to organize Loyalist and Native American resistance to the American rebels for the duration of the war. And despite being a plantation owner who had enslaved African people in bondage, Brown would prove willing to arm Black people to fight against the patriots later in the war.

Brown set up a network of Loyalist allies from East Florida to North Carolina and spent a year living among the Native Americans, winning their trust and, more importantly, forming an alliance that persisted through the war. Eventually, he also raised the formidable East Florida Rangers.

▲ Portrait of Thomas Brown. (*Revolutionary War Journal*, Andy Golden)

was established that they had a common enemy. By now, elite British opinion held that the natives, while "crude" and racially inferior, were also more loyal and worthy of friendship than the Patriots, who were considered rabble-rousers and incapable of any sort of loyalty. They believed that the natives could be trained and utilized in a manner that the colonists could not. In fact, British experiences with the colonials during this period led to an imperial policy whereby British authorities were reluctant to take land from the natives and allow colonists to own private property. This policy even persisted in far-flung British colonies long after 1783.

Lieutenant Colonel Brown's efforts led to the formation of the East Florida Rangers, along the lines of the King's Rangers led by Captain Robert Rogers farther north. In February 1777, Lieutenant Colonel Brown's Rangers and his Native American allies began intense raiding of Patriot areas in Georgia. Lieutenant Colonel Brown's success forced Georgia's rebel leaders to contemplate an invasion of East Florida as retaliation. From December 1776 until April 1777, Southern Tories moved to St. Augustine with weapons and food. This, combined with the raiding activities of the East Florida Rangers, prompted action in Georgia.

The Invasion and Scuttling of Plantations

Governor Gwinnett had begun to gather a force to target St. Augustine as early as February 1777, but several delays ensued, and then finally a squabble led him to a duel with General Lachlan McIntosh in which Governor Gwinnett was wounded and later died.

These internal problems led to further delays and the elevation of Lieutenant Colonel Samuel Elbert and Colonel John Baker to lead the American onslaught.

By early April 1777, Governor Tonyn knew that an invasion was coming. And

◄ Historical marker in honor of Governor Gwinnett. (Author's Collection)

American Invasions of East Florida

▶ Historical marker for Dr. Peck's house, the former residence of East Florida's Royal Governor John Moultrie. It was here that Governor Patrick Tonyn's family had to relocate to once Tonyn's plantation was scuttled. (Author's collection)

▶ The front of Dr. Peck's House. (Author's Collection)

39

◀ A side view of the Peck House (also known as the Peña-Peck House) in the Colonial Quarter of St. Augustine. It was originally built in 1750 during the Spanish period. (Author's Collection)

British officials believed that plantations that would provide aid to the incoming Continental Army should be destroyed in advance. General Alexander Prevost recommended a scorched-earth policy as a result, though ironically, one of the plantations to be burned down was that of Governor Tonyn.

Governor Tonyn, for all his earlier missteps and his previous conflict with General Prevost, proved heroic for the British cause in this moment. Not only did he scuttle his own property in the defense of East Florida, but he strongly rebuffed efforts by other plantation owners to surrender their property to the rebels. In fact, two of these plantation owners, James Penman and Spencer Mann, eventually fled Florida for the rebel city of Charleston after defying Governor Tonyn's orders.

The result for Governor Tonyn and his

American Invasions of East Florida

The American forces of Lieutenant Colonel Elbert and Colonel Baker were split and planned to rendezvous near Sawpit Bluff on the St. Johns River. Colonel Baker arrived at the rendezvous point on May 12, but Lieutenant Colonel Elbert didn't make it to the spot on time. This would lead directly to the first major battle of the conflict on East Florida soil.

The Battle of Thomas Creek and the Landing on Amelia Island

During the first two weeks of May 1777, British forces, including 400 Regulars, Lieutenant Colonel Brown's Rangers, and Native American allies. moved up the St. Johns River and eventually camped close to the Continental forces. At this point Lieutenant Colonel Brown and his Creek allies detached from the main force, and on the night of May 15 raided the Continental camp near the St. Johns River and made off with about 15 horses.

Colonel Baker, feeling under immense pressure, retreated and made camp on the

▲ A historical marker for the battle of Thomas Creek. (Author's Collection)

▼ Artist's rendering of the battle of Thomas Creek. (Artist Kenny Maguire)

family was that they were stuck for the remainder of the war in the small quarters of the Government House and the Peña-Peck House, which today is a tourist attraction in the heart of St. Augustine.

On May 10, American forces crossed the St. Marys River and entered East Florida. Unlike in 1776, British forces were not massed along the river and American troops initially walked into Florida largely uncontested.

The Florida Campaign, 1774–83

night of May 16 near Thomas Creek, on what is now the boundary between Duval and Nassau counties in Northeast Florida. On May 17, led by the East Florida Rangers, the British attacked the American rebels on the banks of the creek. The rebels were ambushed while on the march, many fleeing at the first sight of British Regulars. Their formation collapsed with men fleeing in confusion, pursued by Rangers and natives. After eight Patriot soldiers were killed and many others wounded, Britain's native allies started killing prisoners until stopped by their commanders.

The next day, May 18, Lieutenant Colonel Elbert's forces, who were supposed to be significantly farther south by this time, crossed the St. Marys River and captured Amelia Island, rounding up all its Loyalist inhabitants. After an ambush by Loyalists on the southern end of the island killed one of Lieutenant Colonel Elbert's officers, all residences on the island were burned and livestock was killed. With the Loyalists all captured, the African people they'd enslaved fled southward, and Lieutenant Colonel Elbert decided to press his advantage and drive deeper into East Florida.

As the rebels advanced southward, a naval skirmish took place between the British frigate *Rebecca*, under the command of Captain John Mowbray, and an unnamed rebel ship near the mouth of the St. Johns River. The victory for the British frigate led to Lieutenant Colonel Elbert's forces retreating as they could not navigate the river crossing without being ambushed.

On May 25, after regrouping on Amelia Island, the American forces withdrew

▼ The location of the British during the battle of Thomas Creek. (Author's Collection)

The St. Johns River

The plantations that adjoined the St. Johns River were the most important settlements in East Florida outside of St. Augustine. The wealthiest settlers and most prosperous landowners all had a piece of land near or directly on the river. The St. Johns was the only true "highway" in a colony that was dominated by swamps and inlets. Famous naturalist William Bartram's 1774 visit to East Florida was among his most famous travels. He sailed through the St. Johns River observing alligators, bears, and snakes. He also visited villages and Native American settlements on the river. He noted that it was the very heart of East Florida. This voyage took place only a year before hostilities broke out in the American Revolution.

to the other side of the St. Marys River. Lieutenant Colonel Elbert's initial detachment stayed farther south than the few men remaining in Colonel Baker's force. After patrolling the St. Marys River area for a few months to prevent a British invasion of Georgia, in July Lieutenant Colonel Elbert felt satisfied that the border was secure and withdrew beyond the Altahama River.

The second invasion would mark the deepest penetration of American forces into East Florida for the duration of the war. Colonel Baker had reached the St. Johns River and had been defeated in an area which is now in Northwest Jacksonville. Lieutenant Colonel Elbert had similarly reached the river, albeit much farther east, with potentially a direct route to St. Augustine if not for the intervention of the *Rebecca* in the river.

This was closest Americans would get to St. Augustine during the war, though at the time it was seen as just a temporary setback for the Patriots. Once back in Georgia, planning for yet another invasion began in earnest. This became more critical in the eyes of the Continental Army when the British began to have success with raiding parties into Southern Georgia, thanks in large measure to Lieutenant Colonel Brown's East Florida Rangers and the aggressive foraging of the Seminoles and Creeks.

Third Attempted American Invasion of East Florida

In late 1777, the East Florida Rangers resumed raiding Southern Georgia and even advanced at one point to within a dozen or so miles of Savannah. The Rangers also successfully raided Augusta. Governor Tonyn had been ordered by Parliament to attack Georgia, but for lack of greater force allowed Lieutenant Colonel Brown, his Rangers, and native allies to substitute with damaging raids.

With the raids continuing, General Howe formulated plans for yet another invasion of East Florida. However, this time, he hoped not to rely heavily on local militia and instead build the bulk of his force around Regulars. This was not politically popular in Georgia, and General Howe was forced to use militia in order to placate the sentiment of politicians as well as the enraged public.

Georgia's State Assembly in Savannah offered homesteads and land to induce settlers to the border area with Florida by giving 500-acre grants, but this yielded no results. Residents of Georgia knew that Lieutenant Colonel Brown's Rangers had effective control over the area around the St. Marys River and did not want to risk being ambushed after settling in the region.

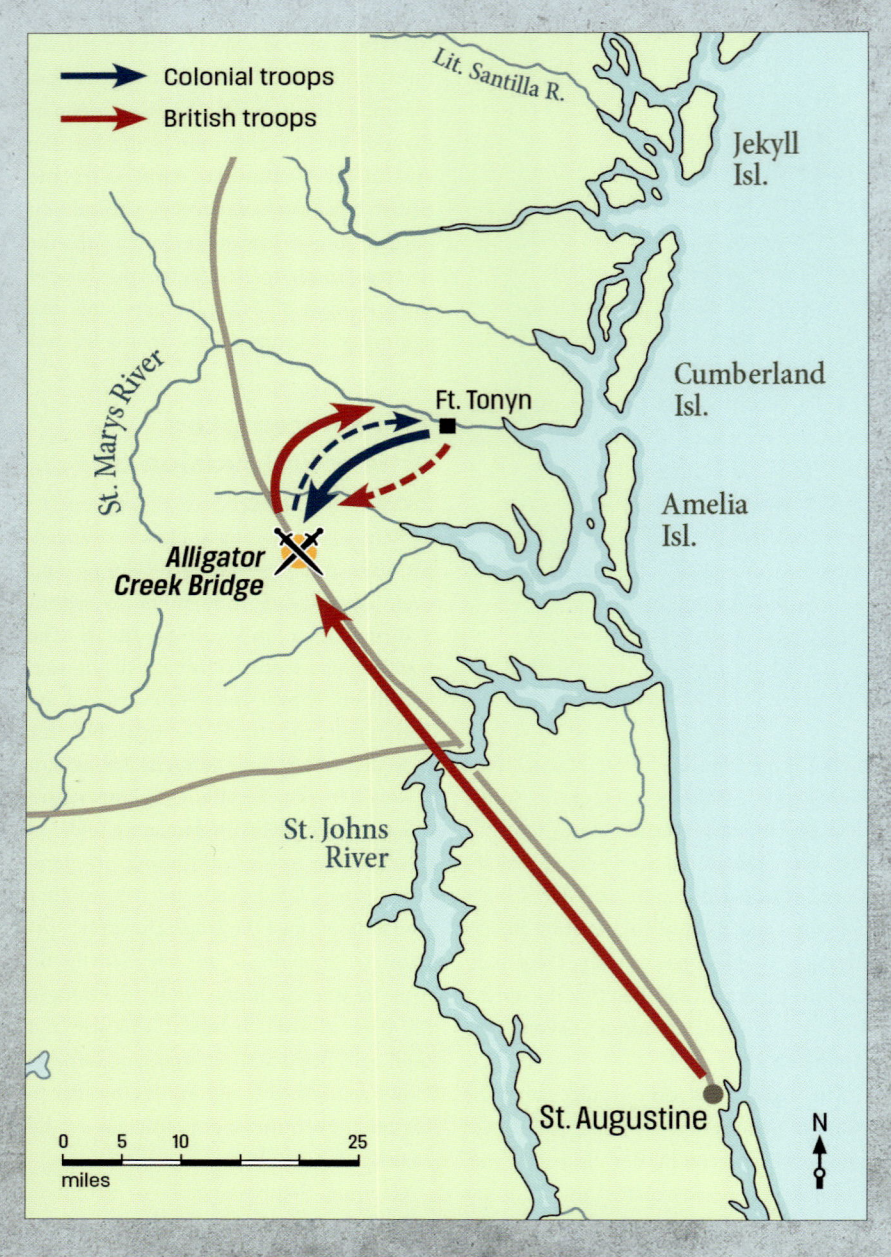

▲ Troop movements leading to the battle of Alligator Creek Bridge which led to the encirclement of Colonial troops.

In March of 1778, Lieutenant Colonel Brown and his East Florida Rangers attacked the militia at Fort Barrington (renamed by the Patriots Fort Howe) on the Altamaha River. The Rangers forced the surrender of the fort and took 23 prisoners. This gave the British a beachhead in Southern Georgia to continue operations aimed toward Savannah, the capital of the colony, which at this point was firmly in Patriot hands. Lieutenant Colonel Brown was even able to travel unmolested into South Carolina to recruit Loyalists there to join his forces. This led to thousands of Loyalists abandoning the Carolinas during 1778 and relocating to East Florida—necessitating the founding of a new town, St. Johns Bluff, which was roughly where Jacksonville is today.

Meanwhile the presence of the East Florida Rangers on Georgia soil necessitated more aggressive action by the Americans toward East Florida for both offensive and now defensive purposes. In April of 1778, General Washington approved a third invasion. The Georgia militia was under the leadership of the colony's Patriot governor, John Houstoun. Together with General Howe's Regulars, the third attempted invasion of East Florida would be undertaken by 2,000 Patriot troops. Lieutenant Colonel Elbert was placed under the command of General Howe and the invasion was to be accompanied by naval action on the coast. This was the lesson learned by the colonials after the second invasion had been halted at the St. Johns River.

A naval assault by the Americans in April resulted in the capture of the British vessels *Rebecca* and *Hinchinbrooke*. The former had been the vessel that halted the Patriot advance the previous year. Three American vessels, the *Washington*, the *Lee*, and the *Bulloch*, had participated in this attack near Cumberland Sound and now gave the Patriots an advantage in augmenting their coming land invasion.

Due to this defeat, Governor Tonyn hurriedly asked Westminster for three new vessels to protect East Florida. He would eventually get them but not until later in 1778.

▼ The St. Marys River today. (Author's Collection)

The Florida Campaign, 1774–83

Battle of Alligator Creek Bridge

In May, General Howe sent his forces south. During their month on the march, they celebrated France's new alliance with the United States with a 13-gun salute but moved slowly toward the St. Marys River. This gave the British ample time to prepare a defensive strategy.

General Howe's forces finally crossed into East Florida on June 28. On that same day, General Howe had sent cavalry under Colonel James Screven after Lieutenant Colonel Brown and his Rangers. After seizing Fort Tonyn on the 29th, the Americans seemed to be having more success this time than in their previous two efforts to invade East Florida. But Lieutenant Colonel Brown and his Rangers were lurking in a cabbage swamp nearby.

Early on the morning of June 30, Lieutenant Colonel Brown prepared an ambush for the Patriot cavalry, and also sent a small flanking force to hit them from behind. Colonel Screven discovered the flankers, however, captured several, and learned of the ambush. Instead, it was the Rangers who were surprised by a sudden attack, and a pell-mell chase ensued, Lieutenant Colonel Brown's men racing toward the Alligator Creek Bridge where they knew that several hundred British Regulars under General Prevost had taken up position. The bridge, which was part of the Kings Road, is approximately near where U.S. Highways 1 & 23 cross the creek today, just outside the town of Callahan.

The ensuing fight was one of the most confused, if colorful, of the war. The British Regulars heard the tumult of battle coming toward them and turned to face it. But since the Rangers and Patriot cavalry were intermixed, and similarly dressed in motley,

▼ Artist's rendering of the ambush at Alligator Creek Bridge. (Artist Kenny Maguire)

◂ Site of the ambush at Alligator Creek Bridge. (Author's Collection)

at first the British couldn't tell who was who in the melee and thought they were under attack by a large force of horsemen. They were finally able to discern that Lieutenant Colonel Brown's men were being chased, so they opened fire on the Americans. The Rangers regrouped and went back in the fight, trying to flank the enemy.

Terrain

The terrain of Northeast Florida made offensive operations very difficult for the Continental Army. As a result, multiple American invasions bogged down in marshy and wooded terrain, which was highly defensible for the British. The two largest engagements of the war in East Florida, the battle of Thomas Creek and the battle of Alligator Creek Bridge, were both influenced by the difficulty of the terrain and the rough, hot, and humid climate of the region. Despite this advantage in terms of terrain, the British took no chances and heavily fortified the region.

The Florida Campaign, 1774–83

The coastline along which the ground forces landed on Amelia Island, present day. (Author's Collection)

After about nine Patriots were killed and many others (including Colonel Screven) wounded, the Patriots had no choice but to retreat. This engagement, which was much larger than the one fought at Thomas Creek the previous year, continued to cost the Patriots, as after falling back to the St Marys River their camp was beset by dysentery, malaria, and other diseases.

Disagreements between General Howe, who wanted to engage the Rangers and British Regulars, and Governor Houstoun, who wanted to bypass the British troops completely and chart a direct course toward St. Augustine, helped doom the Patriot effort. Another school of thought was offered by a militia officer, Andrew Williamson, who wanted to march to the St. Johns River and camp there.

This disagreement effectively split the American forces, and Governor Houstoun's militia were late to engage the enemy—waiting until July 6 to even arrive at camp. In the meantime, they had received supplies but declined to share them with General Howe's wing of the army. Eventually, on July 14, General Howe made the decision to abandon the campaign, as his sick and wounded troops were ferried back to Savannah and the rest of his force marched back north. Soon after, the militia under Governor Houstoun lost their will to fight and they too retreated back across the river into Georgia.

The failure to capture East Florida this time led to finger-pointing in the Patriot ranks, with General Howe and Governor Houstoun sending contradictory reports to the Continental Congress, each blaming the other for the operational and strategic failures. General Washington continued to press for more forces to invade East Florida, but following the disastrous third invasion and comprehensive defeat at Alligator Creek Bridge, political support vanished in the Congress.

East Florida Forces Help Capture Savannah

The Culpher Spy Ring had obtained valuable information about St. Augustine as a staging ground for British operations. General Washington was thus planning another invasion of East Florida for late 1778 but was talked out of it by French General Jean-Baptiste Donatien de Vimeur de Rochambeau, who feared the fourth invasion would go the same as the previous three. As generals Washington and Rochambeau pondered the Culpher information to decide whether to invade

◂ Map of the siege of Savannah. (Library of Congress)

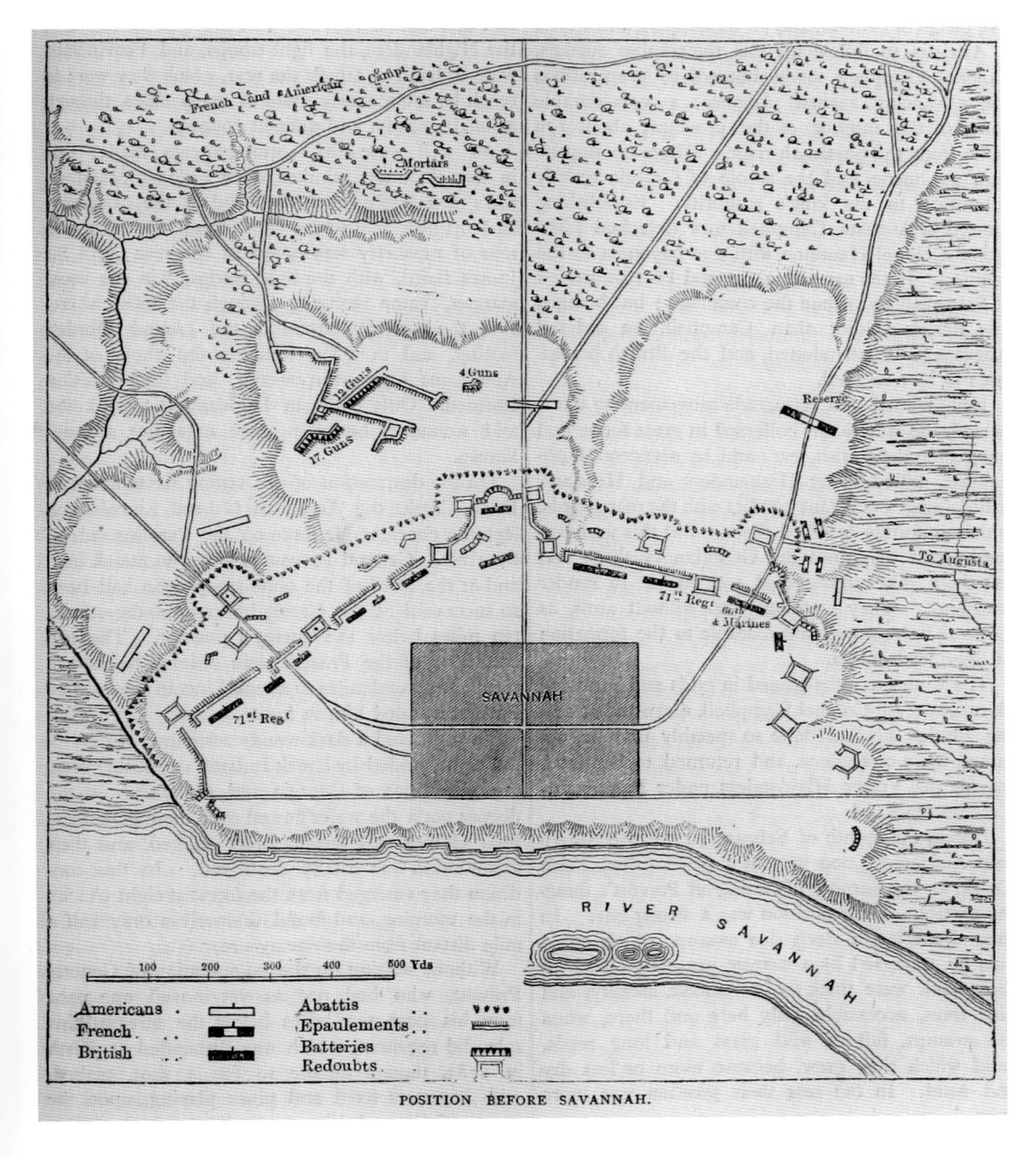

POSITION BEFORE SAVANNAH.

The Florida Campaign, 1774–83

East Florida again, spies informed them that the Crown was taking the offensive. British war planners had chosen to engage more aggressively in the Southern Colonies, feeling that the latest decisive win in East Florida was a sign of Patriot weakness in the South.

In November, hundreds of British soldiers, Native American allies, and East Florida Rangers crossed the border and invaded Georgia. Initially the intent was raiding but eventually due to circumstances it became a full-fledged invasion. General Prevost was given overall command, though Lieutenant Colonel Brown's Rangers were oftentimes a law unto themselves. Additionally, Lieutenant Colonel Daniel McGirt (sometimes spelled McGirth or McGirtt), a former Patriot, became attached to Lieutenant Colonel Brown's unit and would play a major role in these raids as well as future events in the Southern Colonies.

On November 24, 1778, the East Florida Rangers encountered and killed Colonel Screven in an engagement near Midway in modern day Liberty County. The area had already been depopulated, with many of the enslaved and most livestock carried back across the border to East Florida in previous raids.

British troops that set sail from New York eventually joined up with the forces from East Florida, and this enlarged British force captured Savannah the next month.

The capture of Savannah and the ability to use its port as a staging ground for future actions in the southern theater minimized the importance of East Florida from a military standpoint.

Additionally, maintaining Royal control over Georgia meant General Prevost's army stayed put in Savannah, and Lieutenant Colonel Brown's Rangers remained north of the St. Marys River. So this left East

▼ A depiction of the fierce battle of Savannah, by A. I. Keller. (Library of Congress)

▲ The British attack on American forces, by Joseph Derry. (National Portrait Gallery)

Florida potentially vulnerable, and St. Augustine with few defenders.

The irony is that it was General Prevost who had been concerned about leaving East Florida defenseless and Governor Tonyn who had advocated for aggressive action in the invasion of Georgia.

With British troops dispatched elsewhere, Lieutenant Colonel McGirt and his rag-tag group of Loyalist raiders often stood guard near the border creating some semblance of a defense. Lieutenant Colonel McGirt also raided deep into the Carolinas in 1779 with the blessing of General Prevost.

David Ramsey, one of the earliest distinguished American historians, described McGirt's impact: Mr. Tonyn, governor of the last-mentioned loyal province (East Florida), granted a commission to a horse-thief of the name of McGirt, who, at the head of a party, had for several years harassed the inhabitants of South Carolina and Georgia. By his frequent incursions, he had amassed a large property that he deposited in the vicinity of St. Augustine.

French naval patrols were a frequent sight off the East Florida coast in 1779 and 1780, and while generals Washington and Rochambeau actively considered an invasion in 1780, it never materialized. The reason for this was British General Charles Cornwallis's aggressive Southern campaign. The Patriot forces in the South under Major General Nathanael Greene needed all hands on deck to fight off the British forces in the South and could not spare soldiers for another invasion.

General Washington and Major General Greene determined that no invasion would come in 1780 despite the insistence by the Spanish authorities that an invasion of East Florida at this juncture would be successful because British attention was also focused on the West Florida front.

The Militarization of St. Augustine

East Florida's capital, St. Augustine, went through rapid militarization in the period between late 1774 and the middle of 1776. The fear of a Patriot invasion was present until 1780, and St. Augustine went through a huge transformation as a result.

After the American rebels successfully drove the British army back to Boston from Lexington and Concord, British Commander in Chief Gage requested from East Florida shiploads of food and fuel. East Florida Governor Tonyn, a British general,

▼ Map of St. Augustine. (Artist Kenny Maguire)

The Militarization of St. Augustine

happily obliged. But the colony itself was dependent on certain provisions from the mother country.

Commander in Chief Gage was so confident that East Florida would remain loyal to the crown that he dispatched 100 soldiers from St. Augustine to Savannah to help keep the peace in Georgia. British officials had miscalculated the sentiment in Georgia, however, and soon after Lexington and Concord realized that the colony needed a greater effort to be pacified. They were unsuccessful in this effort.

In August 1775, a British brig bound for St. Augustine to reinforce the city's Fort St. Mark (as the British had renamed Castillo de San Marcos) was seized by Patriot forces. Its provisions were sent north to the American rebels who were trying to break the siege of Boston. Ever the Loyalist looking for credit from the Crown, Governor Tonyn had sent many of St. Augustine's provisions north to Commander in Chief Gage earlier in the year, and now residents were effectively without protection from potential Patriot attacks.

Virginia's Governor Lord John Murray, 4th Earl of Dunmore, had also asked for a regiment to be sent from St. Augustine to assist in holding the Patriots at bay. Governor Tonyn wasn't wild about this idea since the city would be left even more vulnerable, but in classic fashion, as a British officer he obliged. As it turned out, Governor Dunmore was still short several regiments and Virginia very quickly fell into Patriot hands.

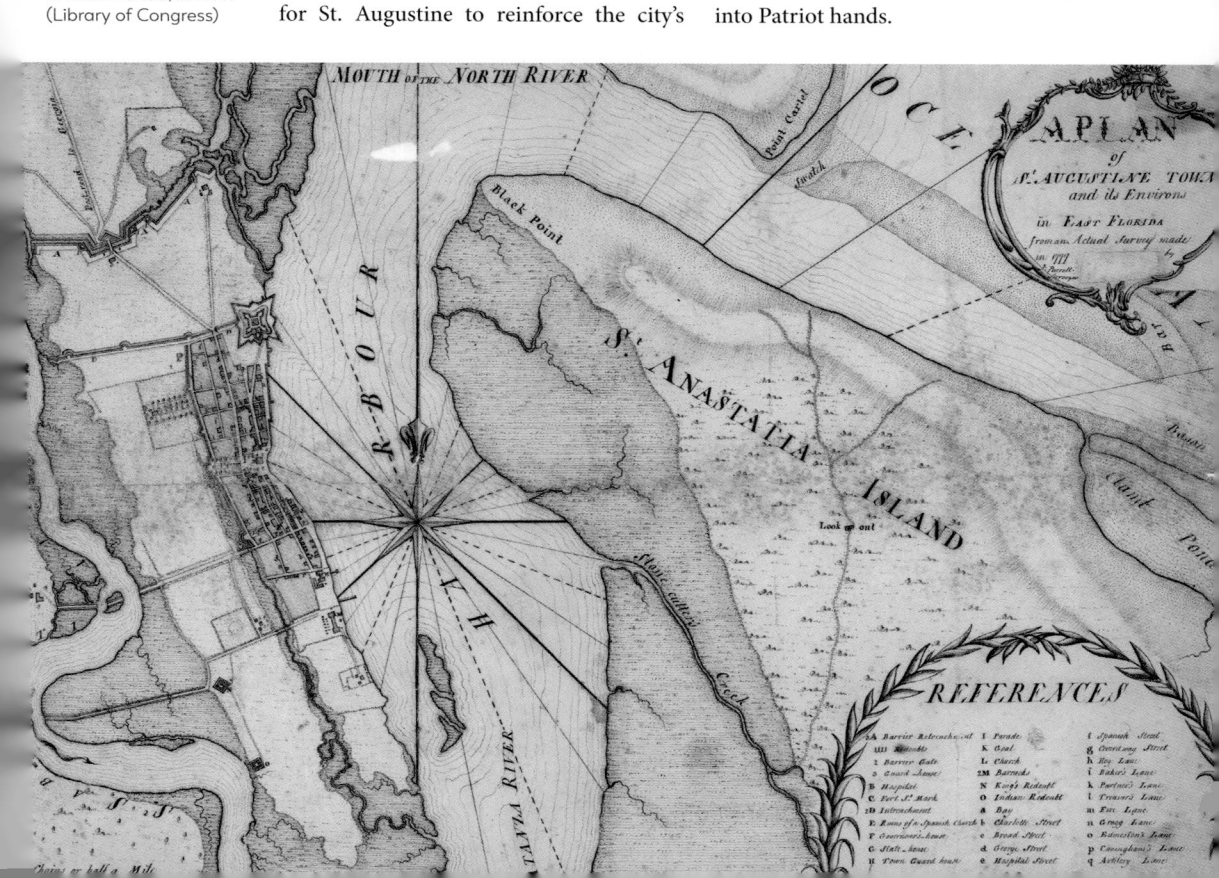

▲ Portrait of Governor Rutledge. (Library of Congress)

▼ A plan of St. Augustine, the capital of East Florida, in 1777. (Library of Congress)

St. Augustine itself now desperately needed to be reinforced. With this in mind, on November 1, 1775, Governor Tonyn issued a proclamation offering refuge to Loyalists from colonies in rebellion. In order to tempt loyal subjects to the colony, land grants were offered up to 500 acres on unoccupied land, but in general these grants ranged between 50 and 100 acres.

By the summer of 1776, St. Augustine was designated the headquarters of the Southern District Brigade. New recruits were coming from Britain and from King George III's German holding of Hannover. By late 1776, St. Augustine was overflowing with armed soldiers and militia, and had the feel of a militarized city.

As the British armed the colony and sought new residents, native allies were also being cultivated.

Arming the Natives

In 1755, the Indian Department of British Superintendent of Indian Affairs John Stuart had prepared a detailed report about the Native American tribes such as the Cherokee and Creeks. While the Proclamation of 1763 angered colonial populations because it protected Native American lands from the Appalachians westward, the areas just east of the proclamation line were filled up effectively with new settlers between 1760 and 1775.

In 1761, Superintendent Stuart was appointed the superintendent of Indian affairs by King George III and worked throughout the next decade and a half to pacify natives and align them with British priorities.

Meanwhile, many of the new colonial settlers that filled up the Appalachian regions were rough-hewn, militia types. They were independent-minded future Patriots, and the antithesis of the types of colonists residing in Florida, who supported more universal British goals.

As it turned out, in 1775 Superintendent Stuart would be forced to flee to East Florida during the Revolutionary War, and he worked until his death in 1779 to build an alliance of native peoples supporting the British cause in Florida and neighboring Georgia. These efforts bore fruit as the native peoples of the areas that were part of Georgia and Florida almost universally supported the British in the war. And as a result, Native Americans played a massive role in the defense of St. Augustine and the few offensive actions launched from Florida by the British.

▲ A street in old St. Augustine. (Library of Congress)

The Militarization of St. Augustine

Superintendent Stuart had lived in one of Charleston's finest homes and was one of the leading citizens of the town. But with the Sons of Liberty in ascendance, he had no choice but to flee after being accused of inciting the Native Americans against the Patriots.

Arriving in St. Augustine in June 1775, Superintendent Stuart found a town in need of leadership, and he quickly emerged as a major force on the colony's leadership council. He, like many others, ran afoul of Governor Tonyn, however, whose conservative style and autocratic manners didn't mesh well with Superintendent Stuart's determination to train and arm native allies to fight against the Patriots.

In December 1775, Superintendent Stuart, along with Governor Tonyn's personal agent, Alexander Skinner, convened a meeting with Seminole and Creek chiefs. The congress was held at Cowford on the St. Johns River about 30 miles north of St. Augustine. Superintendent Stuart treated the native chiefs to a boat trip on the British ship *St. Lawrence*. The conference ended with the native chiefs receiving weapons and gunpowder from the British. In addition, the Alachua Seminoles, who would provide the bulk of the forces, were given beef, potatoes, and rum.

Unlike previous treaties with the natives, which were about land or some sort of conflict with settlers, this congress called by Superintendent Stuart was all about fighting a common enemy—the American rebels.

Governor Tonyn met personally with Chief Ahaya the Cowkeeper of the Alachua Seminoles in St. Augustine, and at this meeting gifts were exchanged as well. Governor Tonyn came away from the meeting impressed by the natives and willing to entrust much of the colony's defense to them. Ahaya the Cowkeeper

▼ The Cathedral Basilica of St. Augustine, a gathering place for the community from Minorca that was relocated from New Smyrna to St. Augustine during the Revolutionary War. (Library of Congress)

left the meeting and headed north toward the St. Marys River where his men would help to wreak havoc on Southern Georgia over the next several years. Governor Tonyn and Ahaya the Cowkeeper would maintain a strong relationship throughout the war.

Key Loyalists Arrive as Refugees in St. Augustine

As the American Revolution gathered steam, additional refugees, many from the backcountry of the Southern Colonies, arrived in St. Augustine. Among the arrivals was Moses Kirkland, a refugee from North Carolina who would play a key role in East Florida's defense, and Lieutenant Colonel Brown, who might have been the single most important figure in the defense of the colony, who arrived from the Georgia backcountry.

Kirkland had been caught in an attempt to pass American plans to British forces in the North and was thrown in a Philadelphia prison by the rebels. He escaped and returned to East Florida by the middle of 1776 and was given a role working with the natives in their defense of the colony. Lieutenant Colonel Brown, by this time, was organizing a militia and was given a full command in 1777.

Governor Tonyn's Miscalculations

At the start of the war, Governor Tonyn proved to be classically misinformed, and wrongly assumed the American rebels were a small minority of troublemakers. The East Florida governor had little appreciation or understanding for why the majority of colonists to the north were attempting to throw off the rule of the Crown. A military man by training, and lacking the temperament for government by consensus, Governor Tonyn created a culture of conformity laced with suspicion in St. Augustine during the early days of the Revolutionary War. His tendency toward authoritative minority rule led to the potential for open rebellion.

During the main colonial conflict, opposition to Governor Tonyn led to a

▼ The Governor's House in St. Augustine. (Author's Collection)

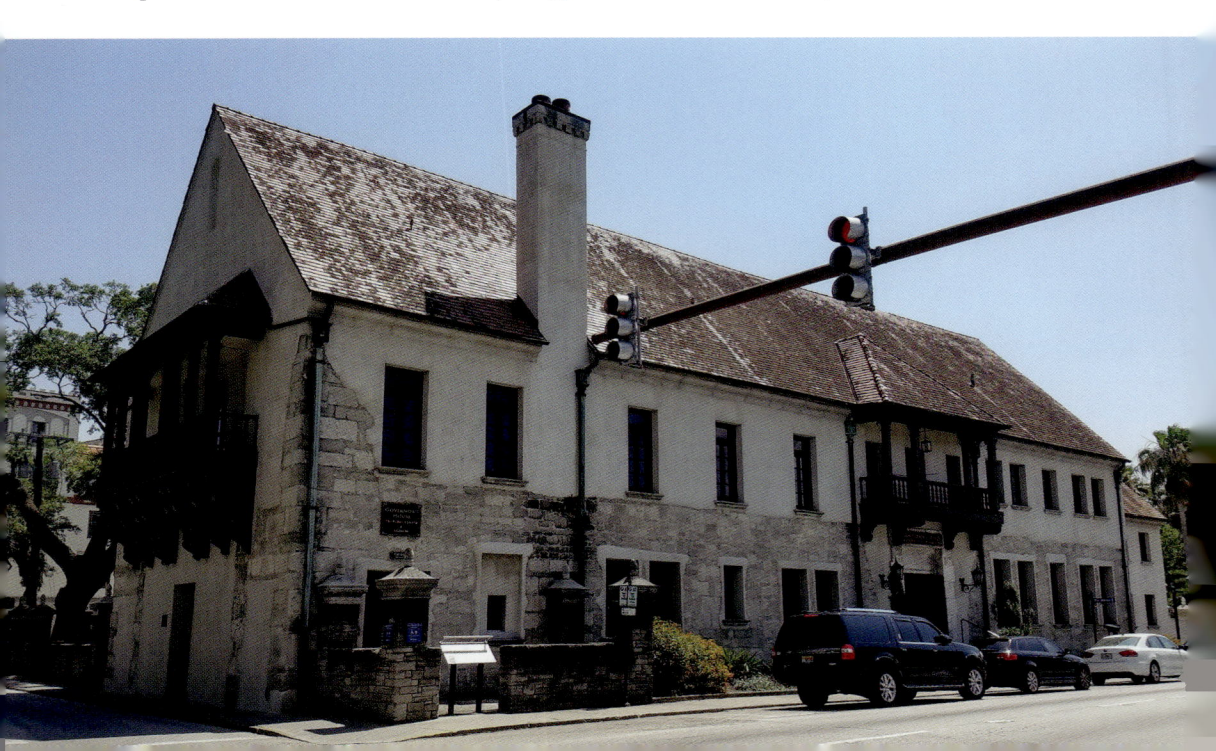

The Militarization of St. Augustine

▲ Aerial view of the Castillo de San Marcos. (National Park Service)

▼ A rendering of the imposing fortress. (Library of Congress)

growth in an organization of East Florida residents that was an offshoot of the Sons of Liberty. This group of about 75 individuals included some of the colony's leading citizens, including Chief Justice William Drayton.

The Patriot movement in St. Augustine appeared to have potential but eventually fizzled out. Many of these rebels would flee the colony between 1776 and 1780, moving to Georgia or South Carolina. Regardless, the Crown's government in Florida had to waste precious time, resources, and manpower to maintain a part of the region they once expected to remain unwaveringly loyal. While the rest of the colony seemed to remain loyal, the overstretched British Empire was briefly at risk of losing a vital seaport, all due to the actions of this one man.

St. Augustine as a British Military Staging Ground

During the Revolution, St. Augustine was a strategically located city whose population swelled thanks to fleeing Loyalists from Georgia and South Carolina. It also provided a security blanket for Britain's more important colonies in the Caribbean from where sugar and rum, and other products, were exported to Britain. Keeping control of St. Augustine was not only essential for maintaining East Florida, it was key to controlling the shipping lanes to the spice islands and sugar plantations of the Caribbean.

St. Augustine was a key to protecting Britain's Caribbean empire much as it had been a key for the Spanish for 200 hundred years to protect their Caribbean assets.

Initially, Governor Tonyn stationed about 50 Seminole Native Americans

The Florida Campaign, 1774–83

outside of the city gates and armed them—they had promised to fight on behalf of King George III. Other Seminoles pledged their loyalty, but leaving the city's defense to natives was risky enough, never mind the reality that they were not trained soldiers. Governor Tonyn raised a militia, but its numbers were not sufficient to protect the city.

St. Augustine during the war swelled in population. In the months after Governor Dunmore's proclamation freeing any enslaved African people who took up arms if they rose up against their Patriot masters, Black people flooded into the East Florida capital, and with the subsequent collapse of the New Smyrna colony and other Tory defections, the town grew exponentially. This was the biggest growth spurt for the city until Henry Flagler came to town in the 1880s. From New Smyrna, 500 Minorcans had abandoned the town in 1777 and moved north to St. Augustine. They represent the oldest continuing community of European settlers that are currently still in Florida.

But the Minorcans, unlike Black people and Native Americans, were continuously viewed with suspicion by British authorities and were as a result not armed or recruited into the city's defense. They did serve an important function as merchants and shopkeepers in a city bursting at its seams thanks to wartime activity. However, some were active spies sending messages to the

▼ Perhaps the most well-defended location of the New World. (Library of Congress)

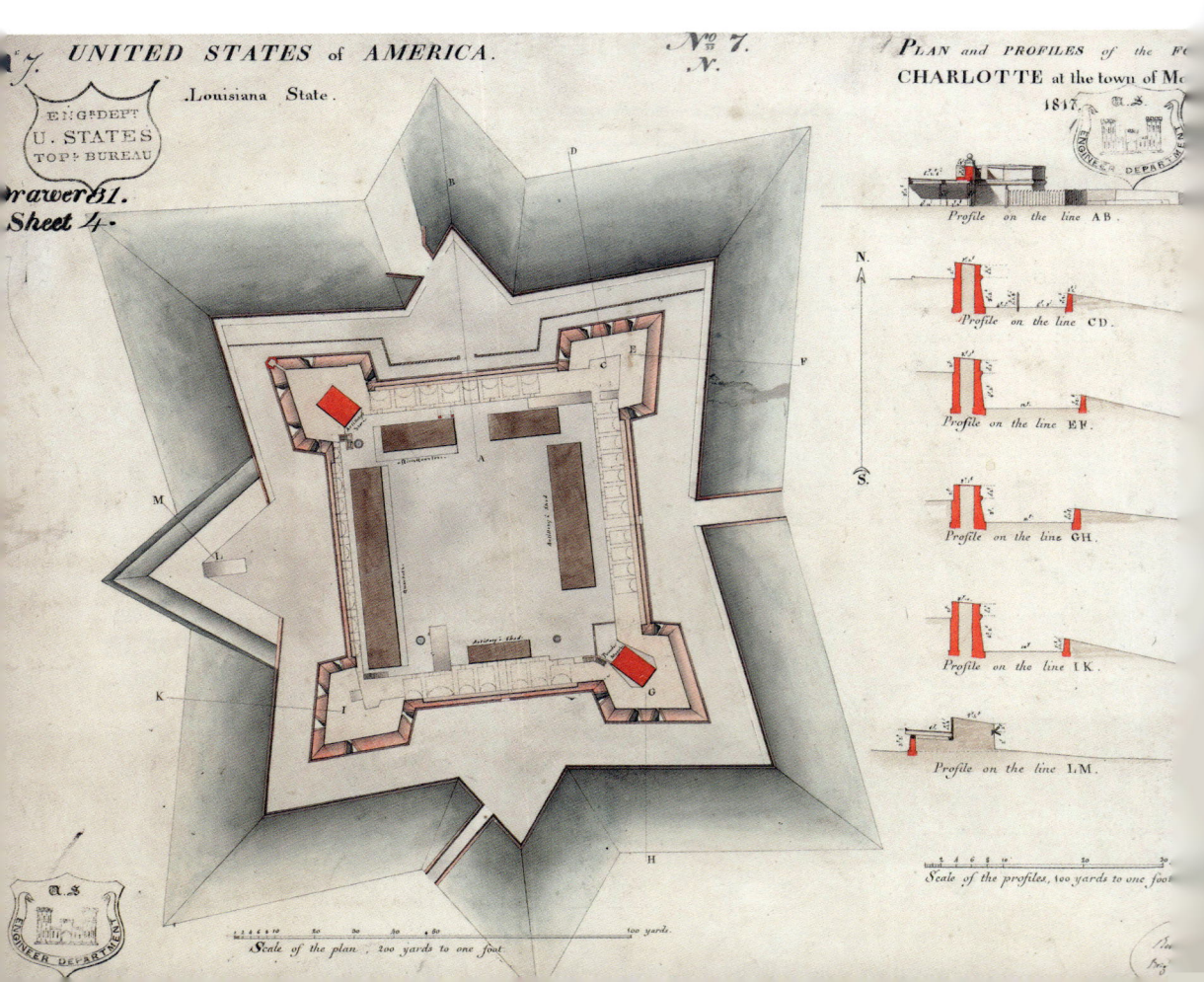

The Militarization of St. Augustine

▲ Rendering of the Fort St. Mark's old watchtower. (Library of Congress)

Spanish in Havana via Cuban fishermen who would deliver "holy oil" to the St. Augustine Minorcan community.

Cosmopolitan St. Augustine

As a result of all this immigration, St. Augustine regained the cosmopolitan feel it had in the heady Spanish colonial days of the 1600s as Anglican Church officials and British officials presided over a city with an increasing number of free Black people, native warriors, Minorcans, other Catholics, and even a small Greek Orthodox community. During this period, St. Augustine became the most cosmopolitan city in what would become the future United States.

Despite this diverse feel, the political leadership of the colony was almost entirely Anglican, meaning St. Augustine lacked sufficient numbers of the Protestant denominations that were more committed to rebellion in the colonies to the north. This also helped ensure that the city stayed almost completely loyal.

Governor Tonyn sent letters to owners of enslaved African people in East Florida asking them who had slaves that could be trusted with arms. While this was risky and largely unprecedented, the fleeing Loyalists that came to St. Augustine brought with them such horror stories about the American rebels that arming every able-bodied male, regardless of race or ethnic origin, became a British priority.

General Prevost was put in charge of the forces defending both East and West Florida. General Prevost was based in St. Augustine and sent regular patrols up the St. Johns River. Due to the British Army needing reinforcements in New York and the Southern Colonies, General Prevost was often undermanned. For this reason he had to look for troops wherever he could find them.

The Florida Campaign, 1774–83

Like most others in leadership in East Florida, General Prevost ran afoul of Governor Tonyn. Much like other leaders in the colony, General Prevost felt that the enlistment and arming of African Americans was critical but at first Governor Tonyn was reluctant to agree. In addition, there were constant personality clashes between them, though unity emerged when many Patriot prisoners were exiled to St. Augustine, something we'll cover in more detail later. Both Governor Tonyn

▲ One of Fort St. Mark's sentry towers as it appears today. (Author's Collection)

The Militarization of St. Augustine

of the Declaration of Independence, were sent as prisoners to the East Florida capital in 1780.

For those prisoners who were given the run of the town, the sight of German soldiers (Hessians) coming from Royal Navy ships docked in St. Augustine was of special interest, as well as the armed native and Black soldiers.

The barracks and military staging areas were greatly expanded around both St. Augustine in the lead up to the initiation of hostilities. By the middle of 1775, a large military presence was found in the East Florida capital. All told, 11 companies of men were raised to defend the colony.

The Role of the Enslaved in the Defense of St. Augustine

Governor Dunmore offered freedom to runaway slaves whose masters were Patriots. Many defected behind British lines in the Southern Colonies, but others continued onward to East Florida.

Governor Dunmore's proclamation and the raising of an "Ethiopian Regiment" supplied with arms and deployed into battle has been given much play in recent historical writings as proof that the British were better on race than the American side. But it must be stressed that Governor Dunmore's policies were not universally adopted throughout British North America and did not reflect official imperial war policy until much later in the conflict. This having been said, we in the 21st century have to grapple with the reality that the vast majority of African Americans who took up arms in the conflict fought on the British side.

There was some concern among British authorities about arming Black people in Florida, most particularly expressed by Superintendent Stuart himself, who was

and General Prevost were also alarmed by the number of enemy politicians arriving in the town.

Initially, close to 30 Virginian Patriots were exiled to St. Augustine in 1776, and later 65 Patriots, including multiple signers

for arming Native Americans but not the formerly enslaved. This debate would rage within the colony until the end of the war, but the course of the conflict dictated less and less reluctance among British authorities to arming enslaved people as the years went on.

Virginia's Governor Dunmore sent many of the enslaved who had escaped behind British lines onward to East Florida. Governor Tonyn wasn't particularly keen on so many freed formerly enslaved people coming into his colony, though he gradually armed them. His reservations

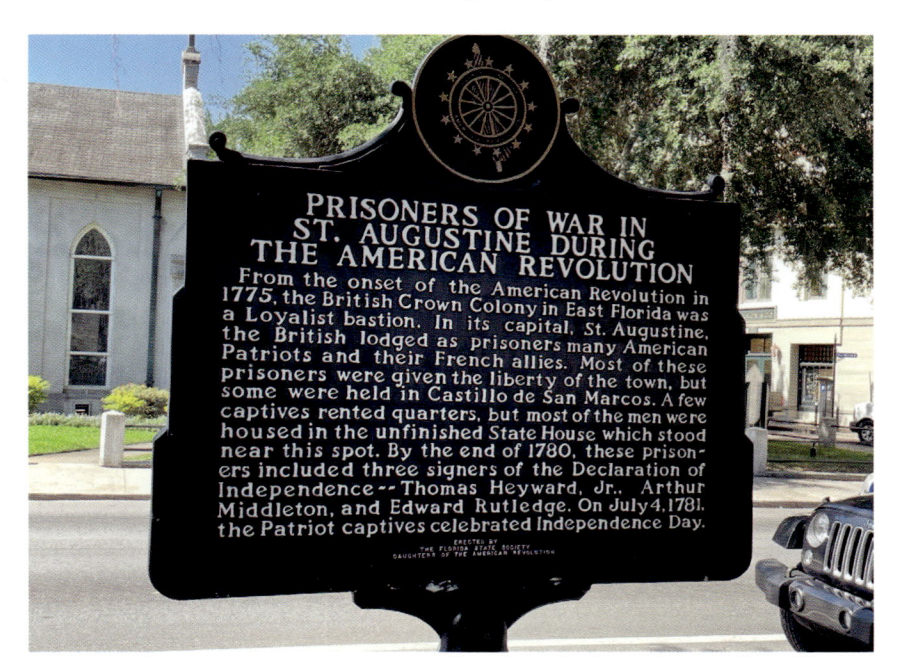

◀ Historical marker remembering the Patriot prisoners of war. (Author's Collection)

▲ This site, Castillo de San Marcos in St. Augustine, was used as a military prison during the war. Note the Florida state flag flying above the fortress today. (Author's Collection)

and that of the other British officials would become moot in 1779 when the British under General Sir Henry Clinton made the emancipation of any African-origin person held in bondage that fled behind British lines an official policy.

But even prior to this point, Governor Tonyn, being the loyal soldier to Britain he was, and sensing the course of the war required the aggressive arming of African Americans, had relented completely. East Florida just did not have sufficient manpower without Black people being armed to create an effective military force.

Most of the fortifications that were erected both in Pensacola and St. Augustine were built largely by slave labor. While in Pensacola this was not an odd sight, in St. Augustine where many free Black people had been armed (unlike on the rest of the North American continent), the use of slave labor in a traditionally intensive labor task not undertaken by local whites created a bizarre and troubling dichotomy.

As the war went on, some of the enslaved ran away and joined the Native Americans surrounding the town. Those caught running away were jailed for the duration of the conflict in a specially erected prison in St. Augustine's main plaza. This however still created confusion because the colony had taken in so many runaway slaves from other colonies who had become free by defecting behind British lines, and were in many cases, as noted above, armed. This made it truly difficult to identify which Africans were still enslaved and which were now free.

In reality, if an African American asked to serve in the British forces, their status was never probed and they became de facto freed as a result. While British authorities varied in their general views of whether arming Black people was a good idea or not, in time it became a general practice. Those who stayed loyal to the crown and served in government in East Florida, even slaveholders themselves, largely came to view pro-independence colonists with greater contempt than any other human beings.

By early 1776, St. Augustine was protected by about 300 British Regulars, 100 militia, several hundred Native

The Florida Campaign, 1774–83

Americans, and several hundred Black people, both free and enslaved. They were reinforced in the summer of 1776 by several hundred German troops, swelling the ranks of Regulars to nearly 800 within the city.

The command of these forces was given to General Prevost, whose clashes with Governor Tonyn we have described above. General Prevost was a Swiss-born professional officer. He dispatched many of the Regulars and Native American allies to posts along the St. Johns River, while keeping German troops based in St. Augustine to protect the city. The Regulars and Native Americans who were sent to posts along the river would prove invaluable in the defense of the colony from multiple American invasions.

◄ The Castillo was renamed Fort St. Mark during its period under British control. (National Park Service)

The Militarization of St. Augustine

Castillo de San Marcos/ Fort St. Mark

Until 1775, the British had left the Castillo de San Marcos more or less in the same shape they found it upon occupying St. Augustine in 1763. The one change was to give it the anglicized name Fort St. Mark. But in 1775, after news of the military actions at Lexington and Concord reached the East Florida capital, the Castillo was largely renovated. By the fall of 1776, the gate house area had been completely redone, and increased earthworks as well as a more robust upper story of the fort were added. By 1779, the outer walls and breastworks had been completely redone, with several feet of thickness added to the parapets.

The fort was thought impregnable thanks to its extensive renovations and became a storage ground for weapons. In fact, the fort proved one of the greatest repositories of weapons for safekeeping the British had in North America. This was something the Patriots were well aware of, though perhaps the number of arms the British had in the fort was exaggerated in American intelligence reports. Whatever the case, the presence of the fort and its stored armaments was a key cause of concern for General Washington and the Continental Army, and helps to explain the constant obsession the Patriot side had with the conquest of East Florida.

But in order to fully protect St. Augustine and Fort St. Mark, troops needed to be sent to Fort Matanzas, about 18 miles south of the city.

Fort Matanzas

In 1742, during the War of Jenkins' Ear, the British had been stopped from a second attempt to take St. Augustine when the Spanish hastily built a fort at a location the British had sailed by in the 1740 siege of St. Augustine. Fort Matanzas was designed

▼ Fort Matanzas National Monument. (Library of Congress)

by Pedro Ruiz de Olano and built without initial approval from the Spanish crown.

Governor Manuel de Montiano, fearing a repeat British attack on St. Augustine, had commissioned the fort immediately after the 1740 siege was lifted, without consulting his superiors in Madrid. It was built at the entrance to the Matanzas channel 18 miles south of St. Augustine. When Florida was turned over to the British in 1763, they found the fort in perfect shape, and unlike the Castillo, no repairs were needed.

In 1776, a rebel privateer seized the British merchant ship *Betsy* off Anastasia Island. This ship was filled with gunpowder and Native Americans looking to join the British cause. The American privateer had been lurking not far from Matanzas Inlet.

With American privateers and eventually the French and Spanish navies patrolling off the Atlantic coast, the fort became ever more important in the defense of the East Florida capital, and after the incident with the *Betsy*, Matanzas saw a regular garrison of about 30 men stationed there throughout the war.

The Royal Navy in St. Augustine

During the course of the war, many Royal Navy vessels called at St. Augustine. Initially the town and its fort was a stop, or port of call, for such smaller vessels as the *Saint John* and *Dauphine*, but later in the war, as the Royal Navy began aggressively patrolling the waters off the East Florida coast, since the French and Spanish were by this point combatants, the capital became a base for multiple warships. The treacherous waters and sandbars around St. Augustine and Matanzas Bay, as they

▲ Fort Matanzas was an important defensive location in East Florida. (Library of Congress)

The Militarization of St. Augustine

The wilderness of British Florida and the site of numerous skirmishes. (Library of Congress)

had for the Spanish, provided excellent protection for the British in preventing any hostile action by sea toward the town.

On the theme of slavery, the number of naval ships that made their way to St. Augustine created even more confusion as many of the sailors enjoying a short leave on shore in St. Augustine were in fact free Black people serving in the Royal Navy. When added to the number of Black soldiers carrying muskets or bayonets in the town, we can see how it became virtually impossible to distinguish free Black people from the enslaved merely by skin color or a distant sighting.

By the middle of the war, St. Augustine regularly saw ships with up to 200-man crews and as many as 32 guns.

American Prisoners in St. Augustine

The city had a Vice Admiralty Court, the only one in the Southern Colonies. Reverend John Forbes was placed in charge and regularly handed out verdicts to the condemned, often those who were contraband of war. This court saw a swelling in cases between 1776 and 1778, and the harshness of justice increased as paranoia accompanied the American invasions of East Florida.

Beginning with France's entry into the war in 1778, French sailors were captured and imprisoned in the city. One captured Frenchman, a nobleman named the Marquis de Bretigny, was kept in the dungeon at Fort St. Mark but eventually escaped. Other French seamen were pressed into service with the Royal Navy, a common practice in that era.

St. Augustine became home for a number of prisoners from Charleston after the British recaptured that city in May 1780. The British arrested 65 Patriots and sent them on parole to St. Augustine in August of the same year. Many Loyalists in Charleston who felt they had suffered during the previous five years of Patriot rule encouraged the arrests and deportations.

Included in those arrested and paroled to St. Augustine were three signers of the Declaration of Independence: Edward Rutledge, Arthur Middleton, and Thomas Heyward, Jr. Additionally, the colony's Patriot political core was rounded up and

The Florida Campaign, 1774–83

Historical marker at the gates of the city. (Author's Collection)

sent to St. Augustine. This included the lieutenant governor, the attorney general, and several elected legislators.

When arrested, the Patriots assumed they'd be thrown into the Exchange Cellar in Charleston. Instead, they were rowed by boat down the Cooper River to a waiting ship, the HMS *Lord Sandwich*, which hauled its human cargo off to St. Augustine.

Most prisoners, though watched closely and with suspicion, were given the run of much of the town. The area in which they were allowed to roam was bounded on the north by the town gates, the south by the plaza, on the west by St. George's Street, and on the east by the Matanzas River.

One exception was South Carolina Lieutenant Governor Christopher Gadsden, who was singled out for insubordination by Governor Tonyn and thrown into the cellar dungeon of the Castillo for 42 weeks. Given the aristocratic backgrounds of some of the South Carolina prisoners, it is no shock that they bonded with some of the local residents. Spencer Mann, a local St. Augustine attorney who harbored Patriot sympathies, rented out a Hypolita Street residence to some of the prisoners. A leading local citizen like Mann was viewed suspiciously by Governor Tonyn. But unlike so many others that Governor Tonyn ran off, Mann was essential to the colony.

Mann was needed and tolerated by the governor because he was among the few financial titans of British St. Augustine, often lending the government money to pay free Black laborers who were needed to secure the town's walls and other fortifications. Eventually the British government would release the American prisoners kept in the city. In July 1781, the middle of the war's climactic year, four ships transferred the prisoners to Philadelphia or Charleston.

British Florida struggled to replenish its numbers throughout the war. (Library of Congress)

The Battle of West Florida

Even after the two attempts by Patriot forces to invade and seize East Florida, many residents of the two British Floridas still viewed a successful conquest as unlikely. Many slept soundly at night, content in the knowledge that they were in a secure Loyalist citadel. This would prove a dangerous and false delusion, for the American Revolutionary War had long since evolved from a localized police action in New England and the Northern Colonies into a major global conflict, with the potential of sweeping every British dominion in the western hemisphere into chaos.

The Battle of West Florida

West Florida, despite the best efforts of the British to tempt settlers to relocate from other places, remained quite small—perhaps about 2,500 white settlers and African enslaved people lived in the province at the start of the Revolution. An effort to make indigo a successful cash crop had failed, and unlike other regions of the South where the British ruled, the plantation economy never quite took hold.

As mentioned earlier, slavery was legal in the colony but was quite rare. The economy developed along what we would later call Jeffersonian lines, with small farmers dominating the landscape, working their own land. Pensacola and Mobile had a market culture, but both towns were significantly smaller than St. Augustine in 1775. Mobile probably only had a couple hundred residents.

Additionally, Baton Rouge and Natchez served more as trading outposts and locations to place small military garrisons to monitor Spanish Louisiana than as true population centers.

When war broke out, the thought was that the large tracts of farmland around Natchez and Vicksburg could be turned into useful agricultural areas for the colony. However, with the initiation of hostilities and the lack of interest from colonists in moving to West Florida, the scheme was never followed through.

Most trade involving West Florida flowed through Pensacola, which unlike St. Augustine never acquired a British flavor. While Pensacola housed a governor and an Anglican Church hierarchy, the town had under 1,000 residents, some of whom were holdovers from the Spanish period, or before 1763 had been residents of French Louisiana.

▼ Map of East and West Florida from Mobile Bay to Apalachee Bay. (Florida State Archive)

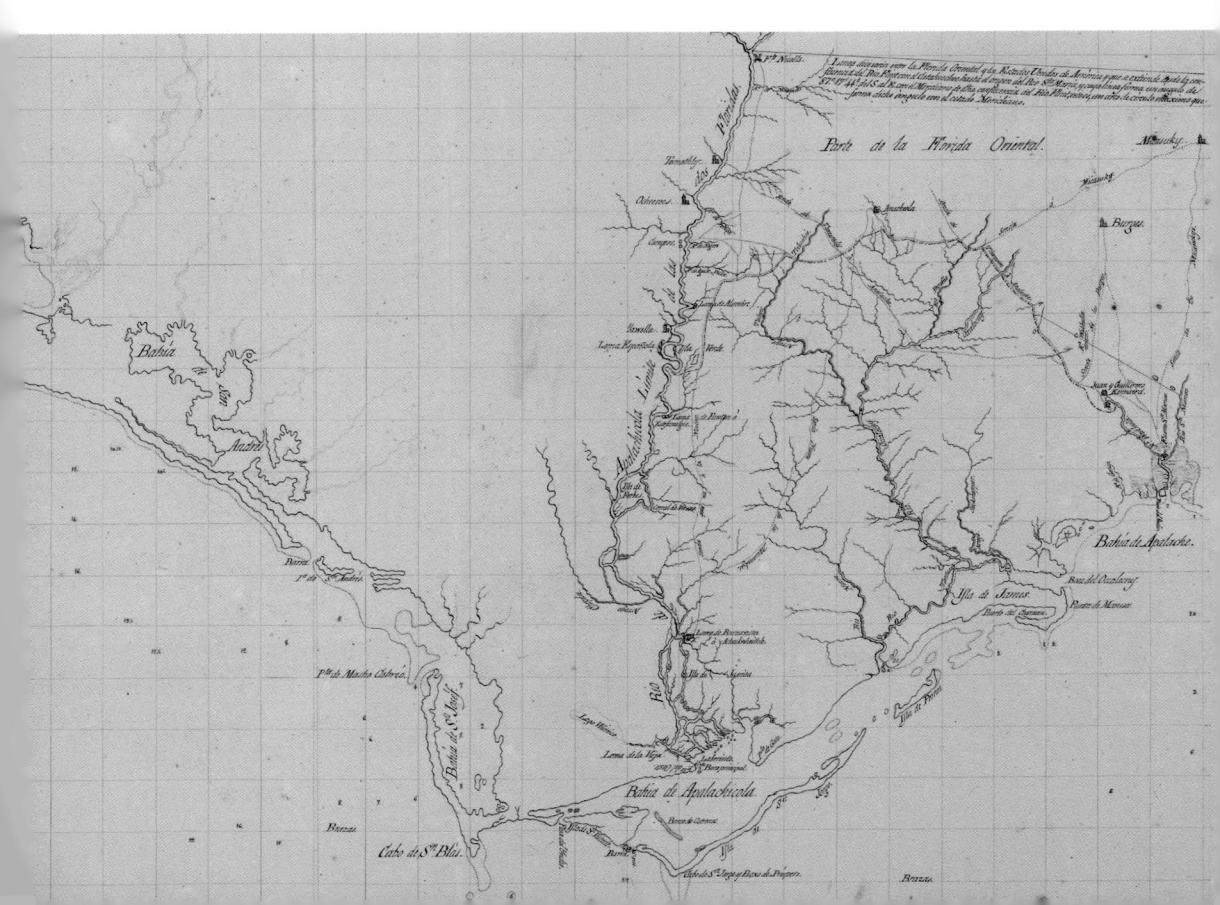

The Florida Campaign, 1774–83

Pensacola and West Florida in general were so disconnected from the British West Indies and other North American colonies (including East Florida) that the area continued using Spanish coins as a de facto currency throughout the period of British rule.

Pensacola was the capital of the colony which stretched from the Mississippi River to the Apalachicola River, which extends down from today's western border of Georgia. It included portions of what are now the American states of Florida, Alabama, Louisiana, and Mississippi.

The British built a fort in Pensacola with four bastions, cannons, and a dry moat. This fort, unsurprisingly, was named Fort George, in honor of King George III.

British Florida Prepares

By late 1777, reality had finally begun to set in on the inhabitants of West Florida. Rumors had started to circulate across Mobile and Pensacola that an invasion by

▲ Remains of Fort Frederica, a typical English fort in West Florida. (National Park Service)

▼ British Florida being prepared for invasion. (Library of Congress)

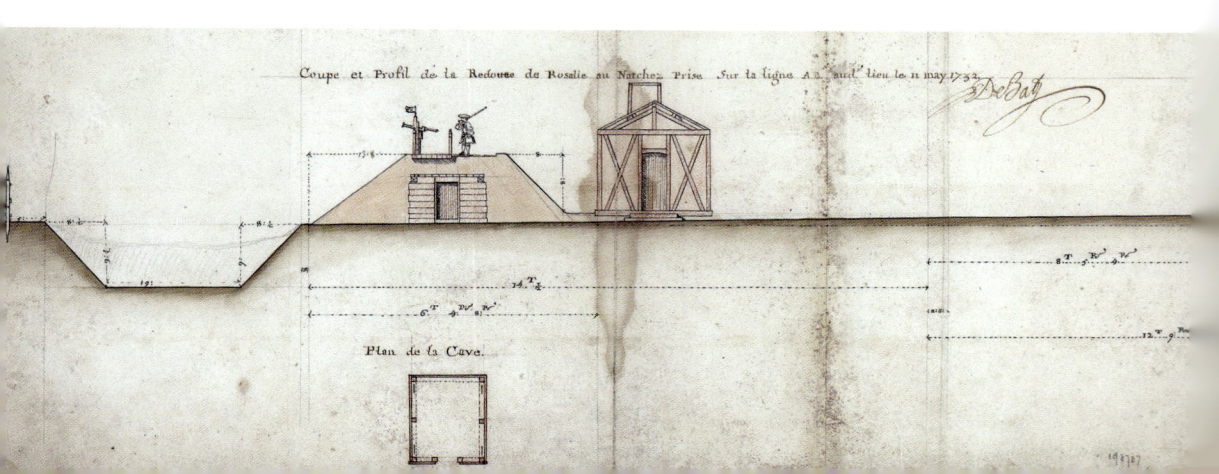

▲ Recent American victories had finally convinced European powers to support the American cause. Shown here is British General Burgoyne's surrender at Saratoga. (Library of Congress)

way of Spanish Louisiana was becoming probable. Despite Britain's unparalleled naval superiority, the colony possessed no meaningful method to repel an attack from the sea. Despite its boasts of having the finest professional army in the world, precious few English regiments were actually stationed within Florida. By the close of 1777, there were less than a thousand poorly trained soldiers in the entire peninsula, much less the territory stretching west.

Relations between the colony and neighboring Spanish Louisiana had grown frosty. In March 1778, the British secretary of state for the colonies, Major General Lord George Germain, had seen the writing on the wall and ordered 3,000 troops to be sent to Florida to bolster defenses. He deemed it necessary to divide the forces between the Crown jewels of St. Augustine and Pensacola. An additional 1,200 German mercenaries and Tory volunteers from the North were also deployed to the region.

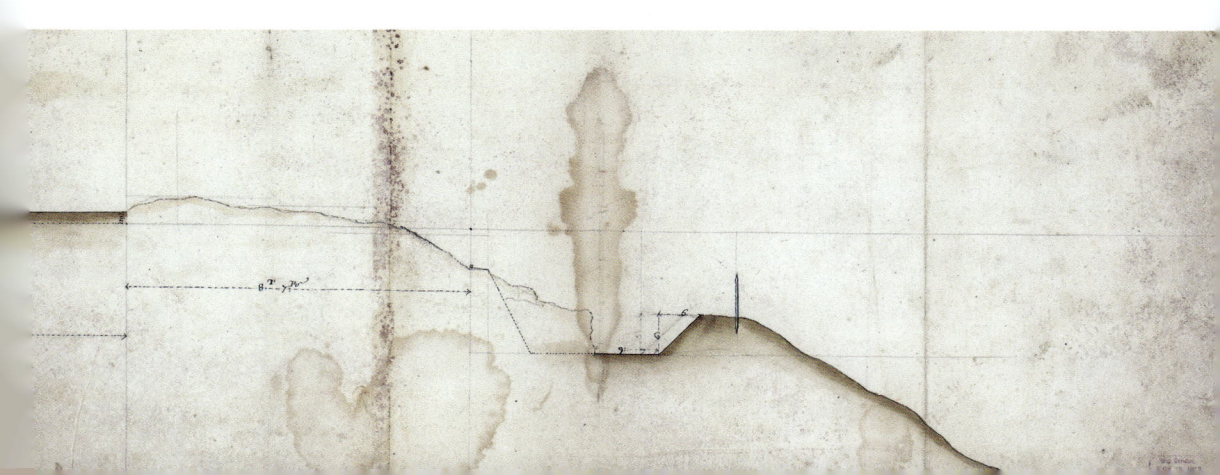

When the new British commander, Brigadier General John Campbell, finally arrived at Pensacola, he was dismayed by what he found.

"Almost a scene of ruin and desolation," he frantically wrote to his superior, General Clinton. Many of the existing fortifications were in urgent need of repair, and numerous sites across the area were left undefended. New fortifications would need to be swiftly built. Beyond the city, the defensive lines were even more precarious, especially along the banks of the Mississippi. Brigadier General Campbell got to work immediately to strengthen the existing defenses, all the while pleading for more troops, more resources, and for himself a better posting.

Regardless of his misgivings, Brigadier General Campbell knew that the danger of invasion was real, and he got to work on an immediate and widespread improvement project. Brigadier General Campbell may have had his shortcomings when it came to offensive strategy, but in defense and logistics, he proved both decisive and gifted. Despite the frustrating Florida weather, which many of his troops complained was unbearable, Brigadier General Campbell was able to draw the most out of his men. All existing structures were strengthened, including a post at Manchac called Fort Bute. Brigadier General Campbell also paid great attention to improving the livability of his men stationed in the forts and took care to keep laborers protected from the region's frequently harsh climate. When temperatures reached critical levels, the men were allowed to rest and finish their assignments during the cooler evening hours.

It was destined to be a long and trying process to build up West Florida. But the British were determined to do so, confident that if the Spaniards stationed

Spain Enters the Conflict

In October 1777 the American rebels had won a stunning victory over the British at Saratoga, and after years of flirtation, the French government had at long last signed a treaty of alliance with the Americans and were openly pressuring their ally Spain to join in the struggle. Although not supportive of anti-monarchical movements, both empires longed to even the score with the British for their losses in the Seven Years' War.

in Louisiana wanted to cause trouble they would be able to make a fight of it. As British forces seemed adequately supplied in the Northern Colonies, Whitehall was now prepared to focus its attention on the southern theater. Both General Clinton and Brigadier General Campbell were hopeful that this would mean more men and supplies for West Florida. They had no idea that the turning point of the war had already taken place, and the British would indeed move swiftly to secure the South. Only not in West Florida. The third attempted invasion of East Florida by the Americans and the siege of Savannah made it abundantly clear that West Florida would have to make do with what it had.

The Carolinas and Virginia had to remain the primary British military focus, with all important sea-based communities like St. Augustine still receiving constant attention. The British could not afford to waste any more men or treasure on the remote, undeveloped lands of Florida.

A Common Enemy and a Common Friend

In December 1776, King Charles III of Spain decided that it was in his nation's interest to covertly assist the new American government. The news coming from the colonies was bad, and the Continental Army was engaged in continual retreats from superior British forces. King Charles III must have sensed that it was a crisis point for the budding nation.

Spain's entire foreign policy for two centuries had been governed by two basic principles: continued access to the Western Hemisphere and taking the British Empire down a peg. There was no institutional enthusiasm or stated sympathy from the Spanish monarchy for the American cause. That would have been too brazen, as they viewed the Patriots' revolt a potential threat to the concept of monarchy and all crowned heads. But they had taken a dangerous gamble against England during the Seven Years' War and paid a punitive penalty for that misstep. Retribution was now overdue.

King Charles III may have felt uneasy when he read the Continental Congress's petitions to King George. Regardless, he was too patriotic to let such concerns stand in the way of reclaiming lost territories. It was decided that the best course of action would be subtle maneuvers, behind the scenes. Spanish Louisiana would provide

▶ Charles III of Spain, seen here during the start of the Seven Years' War, was determined to make England pay for its victory in that conflict. (Library of Congress)

The Florida Campaign, 1774–83

military aid to the new nation. Over 215 bronze cannons, 30,000 muskets, and nearly half a million pounds of gunpowder would be shipped into the colonies, by way of French ports, from warehouses in Havana, and by the boatload along the Mississippi. The Spanish even received assistance from the famed Gardoqui family trading company.

Two Different Governors

Spain also put its money where its mouth was. At a time when the infant American nation couldn't receive loans or establish credit to fortify itself, the Spanish traded with the American colonies and issued loans. Despite Madrid's best efforts to hide it, smuggling from New Orleans had begun as early as 1776. Governor of New Orleans Luis de Unzaga was concerned about antagonizing the British before receiving his official orders from the Royal Court. However, he still authorized the frequent shipment of gunpowder into the colonies. As it turned out Governor Unzaga's actions were not an overreach for the Spanish government, which replaced him with an even more aggressive and pro-American leader. When General Gálvez was appointed governor of New Orleans in January 1777, he continued and expanded the supply operations. He also made no bones about where his sympathies lay. If Governor Unzaga was concerned about antagonizing the British, General Gálvez was determined to do just that. On February 20, 1777, the Spanish king's ministers in Madrid secretly instructed General Gálvez to sell the Americans desperately needed supplies. General Gálvez's uncle, the newly appointed minister of the Council of the Indies, was even more explicit—his nephew's primary goals were to secure friendship with the rebels and to prepare for a possible British invasion.

Britain's Native American Allies

Brigadier General Campbell found himself having to rely more heavily on the assistance of Britain's Native American allies, the Choctaws and Creeks, to defend his province. Both Native American nations proved willing and selfless contributors to the defense of British Florida, despite the muted reluctance of Brigadier General Campbell to rely on them. The governor was not known to shine in their company and seemed indifferent to the nations. Still, the Creeks and Choctaws knew they would find greater autonomy under British rule than under a renewed Spanish regime, much less under an American one.

Unfortunately, Brigadier General Campbell's dismal leadership extended to his inability to effectively utilize his

▼ A map of land along the Gulf Coast purchased from Native Americans. The Apalachicola River at left marked the boundary between East and West Florida. (Library of Congress)

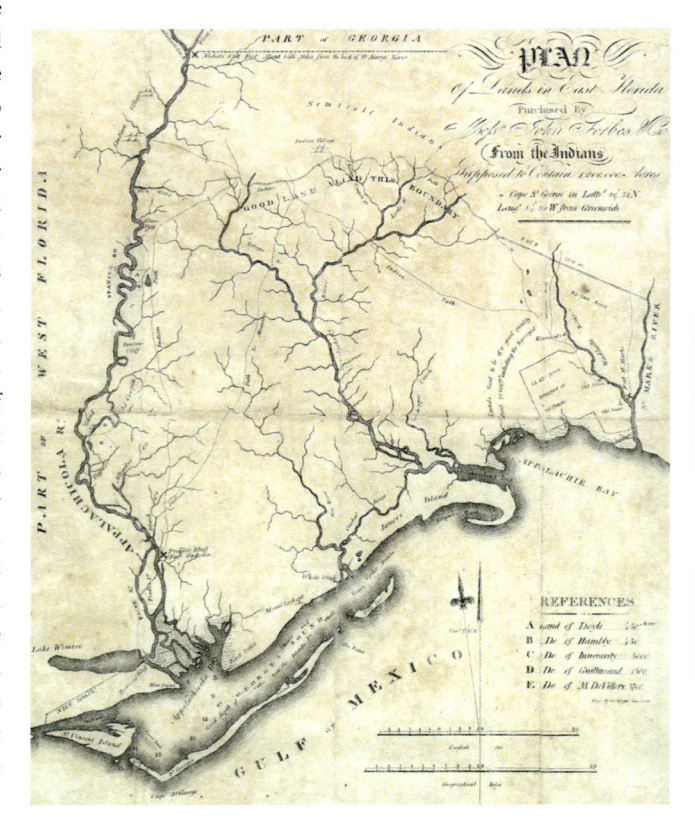

The Battle of West Florida

Native American allies. Luckily for him and British Florida, Native American leaders took matters into their own hands and looked for any opportunity to operate outside of the British defensive strategy. While it's unfair to entirely blame Brigadier General Campbell for the eventual defeat of the British, it cannot be overstated that the Native American nations did everything possible to prevent or mitigate the inevitable. Brigadier General Campbell had prejudiced tendencies toward the warriors even when they proved themselves worthy of praise during the Gulf campaign.

Further complicating the British commander's relationship with the Native Americans was the fact that the month he arrived in West Florida, John Stuart, superintendent of Indian affairs for the region south of the Ohio River, died. London was not quick to appoint his successor, so Brigadier General Campbell was left alone in dealing with the tribes. The Spanish also launched a charm offensive on the Choctaws. One faction among the Choctaws had long been partial toward Spain, and General Gálvez hoped to capitalize on this by sending agents among them in November to distribute coats, medals, and other gifts. When London finally replaced Superintendent Stuart, they divided up his duties among two officers: Alexander Cameron, Superintendent Stuart's deputy at Pensacola, and provincial Lieutenant Colonel Brown. This resulted in a tragic new layer of bureaucracy, as neither man ever felt comfortable talking to tribes to which the other was assigned. The Native American warriors, on the other hand, enjoyed the new arrangement because they received prizes, gifts, and medals from both men.

The Willing Raids

Captain James Willing came from an acclaimed family in Philadelphia. His

▼ Artist's rendering of the Willing Raids. (Artist Kenny Maguire)

The Florida Campaign, 1774–83

1. Embouchure du Missisipi
2. la Nouvele Orleans
3. Lac de Pontchartrain
4. Lac de Maurepas
5. Nouveau Fort Louis
6. Vieux Fort Louis
7. Isle Dauphine
8. Isle de la Chandeleur

LE MISSISIPI ou la Louisiane Dans l'Amerique Septentrionale

▲ A rendering of the Mississippi region in which much of the conflict would occur. (Library of Congress)

father was twice mayor of Philadelphia; his great-grandfather was also mayor; and his older brother Thomas had been a delegate to the Continental Congress from Pennsylvania, and the first president of the First Bank of the United States. Young James was the only member of the family who couldn't find success in his

The Battle of West Florida

The troubling thing about James was that the one thing he seemed to excel in was war. By 1777, now a Continental Navy captain, James Willing devised a scheme to destabilize British West Florida. His plan was backed by financier Robert Morris, one of the greatly under-appreciated figures in the history of the early United States. Without Morris's financial backing, American independence might never have been realized.

In 1778, Captain Willing raided Natchez and plundered several plantations before being caught. He received the tacit cooperation of General Gálvez. It was perhaps one of the first tangible events that showcased to the British the true sentiments of the Spanish. The following year he raided Fort Bute but his raids proved unfruitful for the Patriot side and only led to further British troop reinforcements along the coast in West Florida and an increasing Royal Navy presence.

Regardless, the Patriots did inflict damage to Fort Bute and captured a British vessel there. Captain Willing then advanced southward and took shelter on the Spanish side. His militia formed an information network between themselves and Spanish scouts in the area. Just before the Spanish invasion, his militia forced a committee of local landowners to pledge they would not take up arms against the army of the United States. All told, Captain Willing's raids did much to expose the weakness of the British along the Mississippi, and they served as an effective advance element for the future Spanish forces.

Spy Network

Like any skilled leader during this period in history, General Gálvez had established his own spy network. Trusted agents like his own spymaster, Jacinto Panis, poured into British Florida throughout 1779.

hometown. Despite all his merchant family could do to assist him, every avenue James entered seemed to lead him to unsatisfying mediocrity.

The Florida Campaign, 1774–83

They reported back to their governor elaborate assessments of their enemy's strength, or lack thereof, in West Florida. They talked about the stretched garrisons scattered across the region, the hurried and disorganized rebuilding effort led by Brigadier General Campbell, and the fact that the British military was rounding up private vessels throughout West Florida in order to use them as possible transport vessels for an invasion of New Orleans.

General Gálvez's trust in Panis was absolute, and it was enough for him to begin formulating a plan of invasion. His spies had provided him with all the information he needed to gauge which forts along the Mississippi would be the easiest targets for attack, and he began writing urgent letters for more resources from Havana.

A Common Objective

In the spring of 1779, in Brigadier General Campbell and General Gálvez, the region had two governors of vastly different temperaments and abilities. But each had a similar mission: attempt to fortify a territory surrounded by an enemy, which required constant shipments of supplies and resources from across their respective empires, while operating under a ticking clock. Both men were expecting the other to invade, and both men were preparing to meet the assault.

There lies the singular difference between Brigadier General Campbell and General Gálvez. The former never stopped planning for a Spanish offensive, and simultaneously never mastered the complicated logistical gymnastics needed to properly prepare his territory to meet

▼ A photo of Fort Pickens in Pensacola. Fort life was similar for all nations. (Author's Collection)

it. On the other hand, sometime at the end of 1778, General Gálvez stopped his defensive preparations

He stopped fortifying. Stopped digging in. Stopped playing it safe. He realized that the only way Spanish Louisiana could truly be safe was if it was the one who struck first.

War at Last

All was quiet on the western front of Florida until 1779, when Spain surprised the civilized world and declared war on England, quickly becoming an ally of France against their old foe. The Treaty of Aranjuez signed with France promised Spain a return of Minorca, Gibraltar, and Florida as a reward for joining the war.

General Gálvez set out on August 27, 1779, to invade British territory. Over the next 18 months, he was able to liberate much of West Florida, from Fort Bute to Baton Rouge and Natchez to Mobile, and finally the colony's capital, Pensacola.

General Gálvez was a man driven, perhaps the most fueled by the potential of the new American experiment of any Spanish leader. Nothing seemed likely to deter his ambition to conquer British Florida. Even the sudden arrival of a dangerous and violent hurricane was not enough to hinder or slow his march toward war. The hurricane smashed into the Spanish capital of New Orleans. It destroyed or disabled ships all along the Mississippi and produced negative short-term economic consequences for the inhabitants of Spanish Louisiana.

Still, the aged streets of New Orleans were filled with excitement on the part of the locals, the sound of drums and men on the march ringing in their ears. The governor led his men outside the capital and across the Mississippi. General Gálvez was a masterful commander and a shrewd communicator, and working tirelessly, he gathered to his cause an impressive grouping of French, Spanish, Native Americans, and freed slaves from across the region. From as far as Mexico and Cuba, men rushed to General Gálvez's side to march with him into West Florida and reclaim those lost lands for the Spanish Empire. Madrid had not yet recognized or allied itself with the independent colonies, but General Gálvez saw an opportunity to use these new rebels in his effort to humiliate the British.

General Gálvez's ranks were open to anyone interested in fighting the British. That was the single requirement. As the Gulf Coast campaign went on, his fighting force would attract a diverse grouping of citizens, militia, and professional soldiers. Significantly, his force of 600 Spanish soldiers was augmented by 80 free Black people who volunteered. Additionally, while Brigadier General Campbell counted on Native American support, some Native Americans participated in the campaign on the Spanish side.

As he was building up his large army for an ambitious campaign against West Florida, the general wasted no time in sending a small force upriver to seize the British Mississippi River posts in a nearly bloodless campaign.

Fort Bute

The first British installation to come into contact with the fast-moving Spanish forces was Fort Bute, on the Mississippi some 110 miles above New Orleans. On September 7, 1779, Spanish forces overwhelmed a small British garrison protecting Fort Bute, giving the Spanish control of the lower Mississippi River. The garrison had been led by Lieutenant Colonel Alexander Dickinson.

The Spanish had been concerned that Britain planned to use West Florida to stage an attack on New Orleans, especially given the strong Royal Navy presence in Pensacola. Fort Bute was an old structure, a decaying ghost from the French and Indian War. It was a modest structure only meant to defend the Bayou Manchac, and had long become more of a trading post than a legitimate fort, consisting only of a stockade and an officers' quarters. The whole enterprise could have been accomplished with a handful of men storming the walls. Instead, General Gálvez essentially threw the whole of his army against the small garrison. Only one German volunteer was killed in the brief skirmish that followed.

But several members of the British company managed to escape and made their way to Baton Rouge to notify the division stationed there that Bute had been captured. The six men must have warned their brother officers that the Spanish were coming with an impressive force and meant business.

Battle of Lake Pontchartrain

On September 10, the Continental Navy schooner USS *Morris* (named for Robert Morris), under the command of Captain William Pickles, defeated the aptly named British frigate HMS *West Florida*, which was patrolling Lake Pontchartrain. Captain Pickles sailed with 57 men on the *Morris*, including some Spanish soldiers and a Frenchman as second in command. The majority of the crew was American.

Captain Pickles raised a false flag in order to close with the British ship, and then grappling hooks bound the vessels as

Spain's Ties to Florida

Spain had ruled Florida from 1565 to 1763 and built a strong beachhead to protect New Spain (Latin America). They were forced to cede the colony in 1763 in the Treaty of Paris at the end of the Seven Years' War. Spain had built Florida into a relatively prosperous colony in the late 1600s but a series of wars with Britain between 1702 and 1742 had left the colony devastated. The colony was reduced to two major population centers after 1742—Pensacola on the Gulf and St. Augustine on the Atlantic.

◀ Historical marker for the battle of Lake Pontchartrain. (Author's Collection)

Spaniards and Patriots clambered across the way. Two of their boarding attempts were repulsed in hand-to-hand fighting until the British vessel finally succumbed. The single-ship battle resulted in eight deaths, including the *West Florida*'s captain, but more importantly it weakened British control over the defenses of the colony, opening the door for further Spanish operations. After a few days' rest, the Spanish advanced on Baton Rouge, only 15 miles from the captured Fort Bute. This would prove to be another easy prize, thanks in large part to the military genius of General Gálvez and his masterful abilities in fort warfare.

Fort New Richmond

Built by the British in 1779 on the east bank of the Mississippi River, Fort New Richmond was an entirely different animal than Fort Bute. Built on the Watt's and Flower's plantations, in what is today Baton Rouge, it was covered by an imposing defensive wall of palisades and contained a ditch nine feet deep and 18 feet wide. Over 400 soldiers guarded the structure, including a company of grenadiers, and it housed 13 cannons.

If an attacker thought it would prove as easy a conquest as Fort Bute, they would be woefully mistaken. However, the Spanish had scouted the area and quickly found their silver bullet. The British had cleared the vegetation around the construction site of the fort, but they did not clear the surrounding land. The Spanish would have clear shots at the British inside the fort while they could easily hide among the dense plants, hardwoods, and upland pines. In effect, the Spanish had marginalized the fort's advantages. General Gálvez also fielded a fighting force that was nearly three times the size of the British.

From September 12–21, General Gálvez attacked the British defending Fort New Richmond with both infantry and artillery. The defenders were eventually

▼ Artist's rendering of the Fort New Richmond battle. (Artist Kenny Maguire)

The Florida Campaign, 1774–83

overwhelmed after a valiant defense, and nearly 400 men surrendered. General Gálvez forced the British to give up Fort Panmure in Natchez as well, effectively ceding their strategic defensive positions in West Florida, and leaving the entire Mississippi in Spanish or American hands.

Within a month, General Gálvez had captured six British forts and taken nearly a thousand enemy prisoners. For his part, the Spanish army had suffered only minimal casualties.

General Gálvez demanded and was granted terms that included the capitulation of 80 elite Grenadiers from the newly arrived 60th Regiment of Foot at Fort Panmure (modern Natchez), a well-fortified position which would have been difficult to take militarily. General Gálvez had the British-allied militia disarmed and sent home. He then sent a detachment of 50 men to take control of Panmure. He dismissed his own militia companies, left a sizable garrison at Baton Rouge, and returned to New Orleans with about 50 men.

The Siege of Mobile

At the start of 1780, General Gálvez was ready to push farther and farther into British Florida. His next target was an obvious one, the city of Mobile. It was the largest objective left on the road to Pensacola and was an essential supply point for British West Florida. General Gálvez knew that if he controlled the area around Mobile, he could begin to starve Pensacola.

The Road to Mobile

On January 11, 1780, General Gálvez left his dwelling in New Orleans and once again set out for conquest. He brought with him a force of just 750 men from various backgrounds and nationalities. His instinct was that the need for speed

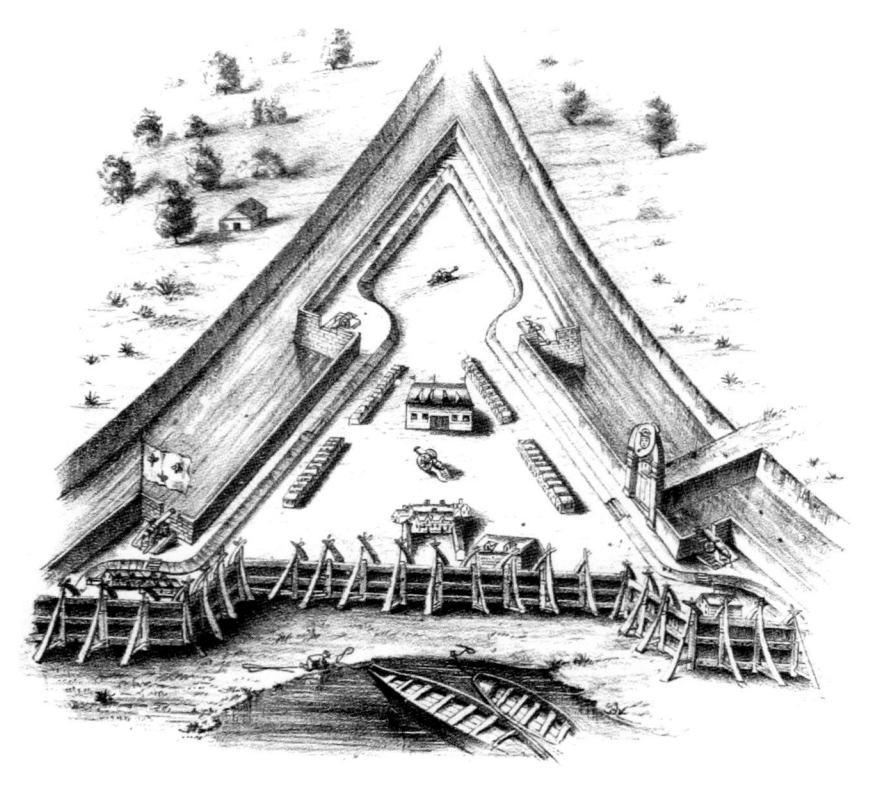

◀ Fort Charlotte at the time of the siege. (Library of Congress)

The Battle of West Florida

was more important than overwhelming strength. He was determined to reach Mobile quickly. The force traveled by boat down the Mississippi River and into the Gulf until they reached Mobile Bay in early February.

Once again, the unpredictable weather batted for England and a sudden winter storm along the Gulf delayed their arrival.

They made landfall on Mobile Point and unloaded some of their ships' 2-ton guns for a future battery. Five ships from Havana arrived at Mobile Point with over 1,400 men and a mountain of supplies and equipment. The Spanish force now moved farther north past Mobile Bay and reached the outskirts of the city. Finally, they reached the heart of the British defenses, Fort Charlotte.

▼ A replica of Fort Charlotte. (Author's Collection)

The Strange Civility of War

One of the great marvels of this siege was the manner in which the two opposing commanders conducted themselves. They were warriors, of course, but they were also gentlemen and men of honor. Former West Florida Governor Elias Durnford was the commanding officer of Fort Charlotte. When General Gálvez made landfall he dispatched one of his officers, the Lieutenant Governor of Louisiana Francisco Bouligny, to meet with their opponent.

Riding under a white flag, Lieutenant Governor Bouligny was granted safe passage and an audience with the former governor. Any uninformed outsider would have assumed they were polite colleagues and not mortal enemies determined to destroy one another. Lieutenant Governor Bouligny delivered a message written in General Gálvez's hand asking for the peaceful surrender of the fort. General Gálvez laid out his case in the most earnest and sincere manner possible; the Spanish had more men, and British reinforcements from Pensacola wouldn't arrive in time. Durnford processed the message and admitted that General Gálvez's points were valid. But it would be unthinkable for him to surrender the fort and the city.

Fair enough! The two men then cut off early and retired to Durnford's private quarters. There they enjoyed a wonderful meal and drank glasses of elegant wine. They took turns toasting their respective sovereign's health.

When the siege began, this odd dynamic continued between conqueror and defender. General Gálvez and Durnford exchanged gifts with each other, engaging in an odd parallel competition while the siege was taking place. They were determined to one-up the other's kindness.

The Florida Campaign, 1774–83

Durnford sent General Gálvez a dozen chickens and bottles of wine; General Gálvez sent a case of Bordeaux and a box of oranges. Durnford sent letters requesting fair treatment of his men along with fresh bread for General Gálvez; Durnford received tea cakes and Havana cigars.

Fort Charlotte

Intelligence reports from the year before had pointed out that Fort Charlotte, the defensive key to Mobile, was still undergoing slow repairs. It would be structurally vulnerable to attack. The hostile climate of the region was also causing many of the fort's defenders to take to bed with chronic fatigue or illness. General Gálvez seemed confident that he could overrun the enemy with a decisive attack before reinforcements from the colony's capital could arrive.

Once the Spanish unloaded from their ships, they began the slow march toward the fort, carrying with them heavy artillery. In March the general reached the town of Mobile and began a brutal assault on the community. The inhabitants and British soldiers put up a brave resistance and held out for as long as they could. The Spanish vessel *Valenzuela* had been firing its 24-pounder cannon onto the town since late February. By the time the main bulk of General Gálvez's forces had arrived, the town was softened up.

The Spanish moved on Mobile with 7,500 Regulars and militia. The British delayed sending large-scale military support from Pensacola, but eventually 3,500 troops defended Mobile and Fort Charlotte. At twilight on March 12, 1780, a flag of truce was raised over the fort and all guns went silent. The British had requested

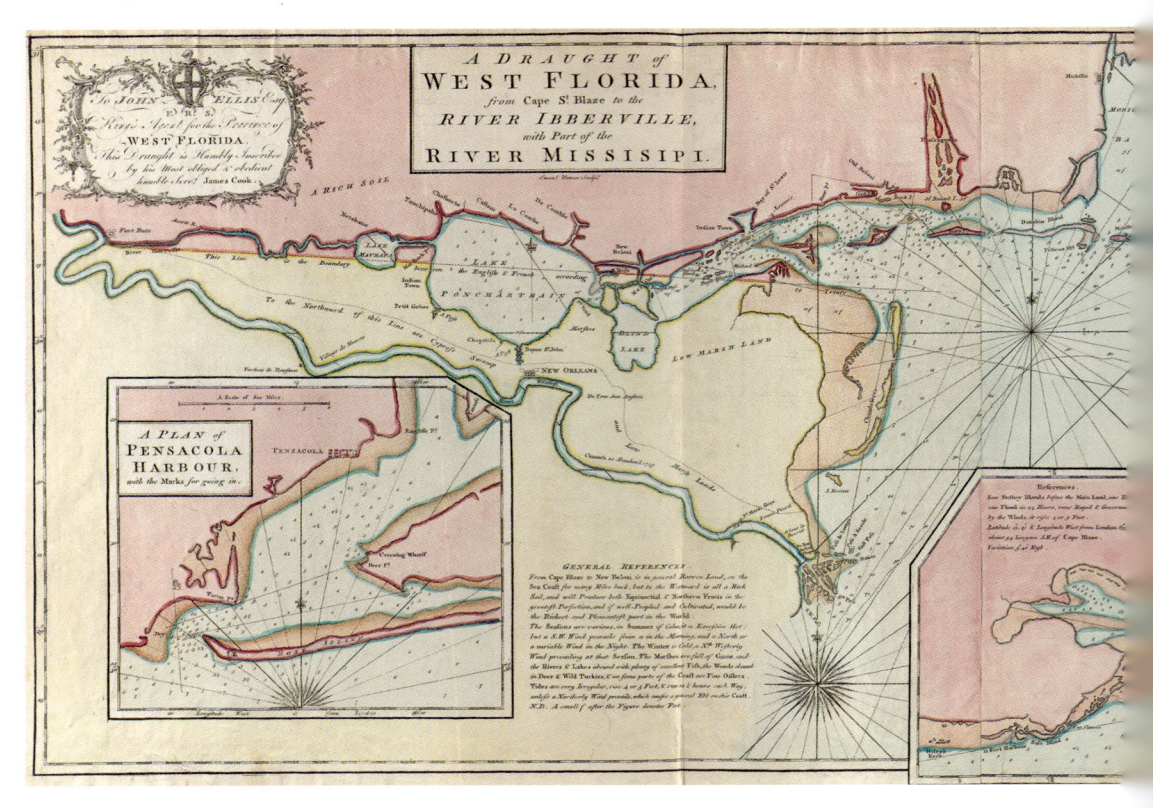

The Battle of West Florida

▶ Fort Charlotte was an imposing structure for the Spanish army. (Author's Collection)

a ceasefire and offered a surrender of the fort. Durnford, sensing that General Gálvez was a gentleman, requested that in return for the surrender of the fort he and his men be allowed to leave the area and return to Pensacola. Since the capital was his next target, this was something that General Gálvez could not allow, and he flatly denied the request. The British would have to surrender and the garrison's inhabitants be made prisoners of war or the siege would continue.

Fort Charlotte fell on March 13, and Mobile was captured the next day. Governor Durnford was taken as a prisoner. Based on the budding friendship between himself and General Gálvez, however, it must have been imprisonment with tea cakes and full-bodied wine.

◀ A map of West Florida with a close-up view of Pensacola Harbor. (Florida State Archives)

87

The Gulf Coast Campaign

The Gulf campaign and its centerpiece, the siege of Pensacola, has largely been ignored in most accounts of the American Revolution. It was the climactic and triumphant moment in a forgotten theater of the war. Since the chief players were largely European, there have been more than a few colonial historians over the years who have not even regarded it as an actual part of the American struggle for independence. Still, it was an important event in the war, and a turning point for both America and the empires of Europe.

Pensacola was a relatively small community in 1781, much more so than its East Florida counterpart, St. Augustine. The chief marvel of the community was its defenses: Fort George, which overlooked the town; and two outworks, known as the Prince of Wales and Queen's redoubts. There was also another, less impressive fortification, Red Cliffs Fort, by the mouth of Pensacola Bay. The town contained around 200 frame houses and several modest government buildings—nothing elaborate, which was a common feature of most communities in this part of the empire. Forts were the palaces; they were just as vital as the land they rested on.

▼ *A Perspective View of Pensacola.* This drawing was published in 1764, shortly after Pensacola was named the capital of British West Florida. (Library of Congress)

The Gulf Coast Campaign

▲ Continental Army Commander in Chief George Washington, shown here, was committed to conquering Florida even during the later stages of the war. (Library of Congress)

General Gálvez was close to obsessive about reclaiming Pensacola for Spain. Even as he accepted the British surrender of Fort Charlotte, his gaze was already fixed on the city. On the other side, the shadow of a Spanish invasion was something felt throughout the community, a looming danger over daily life.

The Plan

The successful capture of Pensacola would be no easy task, for the city was without question the best fortified in the region. It was manned by a well-equipped garrison, centered at the very heart of the city. The only way an invading army could even access the city was through a narrow harbor entrance that was protected by a British flotilla.

There was a serious risk that even if General Gálvez managed to capture Pensacola, his fighting strength might be so weakened by the undertaking that he no longer would have the strength to stay in the field. There was also the fact that the British seemed to be expecting him to lay siege. Spies had confirmed as much. Local townspeople and government officials donated supplies and funds to help build numerous defensive structures and barriers across the city. The reasonable goal of this ambitious building project was to protect the eastern and western sides of the city from possible attack.

At least one wealthy landowner in the area fortified his plantation with a stockade and artillery so that residents could take an active part in the defense. Stockpiles for a long siege had been gathered, enough to keep the community fed; and a force of 2,000 British soldiers and 1,000 Native American allies were stationed within the town. Hopothle Mico, or the Talassee King of the Creeks, had sided with the British, and his tribe helped to defend Pensacola during the Spanish siege.

The Florida Campaign, 1774–83

◀ Hopothle Mico, or the Talassee King of the Creeks. (Library of Congress)

Campbell's Error

Brigadier General Campbell was in command of the recently completed Fort George, and had at his disposal several companies of the 16th and 60th Regiments of Foot, a battalion of Hessians, and two motley battalions of American Loyalists recruited from Maryland and Pennsylvania—a total of nine hundred men.

Then Brigadier General Campbell made a tragic miscalculation. Either through complacency or just pure delusion, he seemed to find false security in the fortifications of the town. He felt too much comfort for any military leader who was supposed to be digging in for a long fight. He lost his siege mentality and began acting strangely confident that the Spanish wouldn't invade after all. Even as the Spanish fleet massed off Santa Rosa Island, the English general did not believe they would attack.

He failed to grasp the importance of Pensacola as the key to naval supremacy in the Gulf of Mexico. Maintaining it would be the only way the British could ever reclaim the West Florida territories they had already lost.

Aftermath of Mobile

The British flag had been lowered over Fort Charlotte and every other former British stronghold west of Pensacola. General Gálvez was now the governor of Louisiana and Mobile. He appointed a veteran, Colonel José de Ezpeleta y Galdeano, to command the fort at Mobile and fortify the surrounding areas for a possible British counterattack. General Gálvez set off for New Orleans and left 700 men behind to defend the conquered territory.

Ezpeleta's mission was clear. The Spanish had overextended themselves, and General Gálvez needed to organize a second offensive against the remainder of British West Florida. Ezpeleta had to pacify the locals and begin making overtures to the Creeks and Choctaws. If the Spanish could prevent these tribes from attacking Mobile on behalf of the British, all of Ezpeleta's energies could be focused on firmly establishing Spanish dominance over the area.

It was wishful thinking. The British would make the Spanish see just how difficult it was to defend so much territory with limited resources. Throughout the summer and fall, skirmishes between the two sides were frequent.

Battle at the Village

In January 1781, the British, along with their Native American allies, attempted to recapture Mobile. The concern was that if they recaptured the town, they could threaten New Orleans. A force of about 350 British Regulars, plus Loyalist units and close to 500 native allies, made their way toward Mobile.

The effort went to naught, however, as on January 7, 200 Spanish Regulars defeated the force of close to 850 British troops and Native American allies. A garrison was left behind to deter further British attacks as General Gálvez began to move the majority of his forces toward an attack on Pensacola, the big prize of the Gulf campaign.

While the British had been retreating throughout the Gulf Coast, they had little intention of giving up Pensacola without a serious fight. It was obvious the Spanish wouldn't stop until they had captured Pensacola, and it was becoming clear that the British were willing to sacrifice most of the Gulf Coast in exchange for a solid defense of West Florida's capital.

With the Spanish victory at Mobile, Fort Charlotte was garrisoned with Spanish troops, and a second fort was built over the next few months across from Mobile Bay. Referred to as the "Spanish Fort," this locale became the spot for General Gálvez to regroup and strategize in preparation for a massive attack on Pensacola. He made a quick decision that some of the regular troops from New Orleans needed rest following their long march. Many of them would be left behind to garrison the two new forts. To repopulate his ranks General Gálvez sought out troops and fresh supplies from Havana, Cuba.

A Troubled Start

In March 1781, Captain José Calvo de Irázabal brought the Spanish fleet from Havana to the mouth of Pensacola Bay to initiate the siege. After nine long days at sea, the fleet arrived at the island of Santa Rosa, outside the bay. The entrance to the bay was defended by the fort of San Carlos on the continental side and a battery of cannon on the island of Santa Rosa.

When General Gálvez landed his troops on Santa Rosa Island it must have been an awesome sight. There were great ships-of-the-line, frigates, and a number of smaller, recently captured vessels used as lighters to land provisions and troops onto the beach.

The Florida Campaign, 1774–83

Perhaps more than 64 ships and over 5,000 troops landed on Santa Rosa Island.

The Spanish easily drove off the British troops on one side of the island, removing the threat of a dangerous British crossfire and allowing the flagship of the fleet to enter the bay. The ship was commanded by the chief of the naval force, Captain de Irázabal. At first, it looked as though the ship was going to pass the fort when it suddenly ran partially aground on a sandbank.

Cannon fire was landing closer and closer to the trapped vessel, and the crew had to work quickly to prevent catastrophe. Fortunately, the ship managed to escape unscathed, and the entire armada retreated back to safety. Nevertheless, the episode unnerved Captain de Irázabal and he forbade any ship to pass through the mouth of the bay again. He and General Gálvez exchanged letters with harsh words and accusations over the next few days. General Gálvez tried to persuade and then pressure the naval commander to relent and renew the attack.

The situation was slipping away for General Gálvez. Conditions for his men

Profile:
General Bernardo de Gálvez (1746–86)

General Gálvez was the colonial governor of Spanish Louisiana and Cuba. He would later become the viceroy of New Spain. While governor of Louisiana, Gálvez developed a trade policy that sought to limit economic interaction with the British colonies in North America.

Prior to Spain's formal entry into the war, he was in contact with the Continental Congress and helped guide the Spanish Crown toward a more pro-American policy. Gálvez even helped facilitate American raiding on British ships, though at the time Spain was still neutral. Once Spain entered the war in 1779, Gálvez was free to pursue a conquest of West Florida.

A legend in his own time as a spirited and tenacious military leader who achieved several decisive victories in the Gulf campaign, this man of action who bearded the British lion died in 1786 at the age of 40, from typhus.

▲ General Gálvez is regarded as one of the great heroes of the American Revolution. (National Portrait Gallery)

The Gulf Coast Campaign

would soon deteriorate, and the unpredictable Gulf weather was beginning to turn poor. If the army and naval leadership couldn't come to some agreement the ships would put to sea and the expedition would be a failure. This was the moment to seize the capital of West Florida, and General Gálvez knew it. If they couldn't push through, it would be months before another advance could be mounted. That would only give the British time to strengthen their defenses.

When Gálvez protested again, the naval officers all stood united—they weren't going to risk their ships and their sailors over the governor's determination to take Pensacola. There wasn't much for General Gálvez to do. He was the commander of the army, but he did not have control of the Spanish navy. The ships could not be made to move through Pensacola Bay if their commanding officers all thought it was too dangerous.

But of course, General Gálvez was not defeated for long. He still had control of his own ship and three others from New Orleans. He would take these few vessels into the Bay.

"I Alone"

This moment would be called General Gálvez's finest hour, and it would make him a legend. Accounts vary, and like many events in history, they have been amended or revised with time. But all accounts agree that General Gálvez placed himself before the men on his flagship and declared, "Whoever has honor and courage, follow me!" Later on, the tale and the speech grew with the retelling and the speech became grander: "I, my sons, went alone to sacrifice!"

After observing the offloading of cannons and gunpowder from British ships, General Gálvez had his little flotilla sail into Pensacola Bay under a hail of

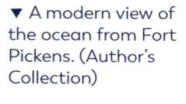

▼ A modern view of the ocean from Fort Pickens. (Author's Collection)

The Florida Campaign, 1774–83

gunfire from the British redoubt. The Spanish naval commanders had been worried about the damage their ships would suffer from the cannon fire of the British. They must have been frozen in silence, speechless, as shot after shot failed to reach General Gálvez's ships. His standard was raised, mocking his enemies and challenging his allies to follow him.

They did! The British cannon shots failed to reach a single Spanish ship, and despite the strength of Pensacola's defenses they were not enough to prevent a Spanish landing. Eventually Gálvez's personal motto became "*Yo Solo*" or "I alone." It would become an essential part of his mythical stature in Spain, and King Charles agreed to honor General Gálvez by letting the motto be included on his personal coat of arms.

Settling into Position

By the end of March, the British and Spanish had settled into their respective positions. General Gálvez began to consolidate troops on the mainland outside of the city, and gradually his army established what would be its main camp northeast of Bayou Chico. British scouts observed their activities and began planning a large counterattack on the camp to force them off the mainland before their reinforcements could arrive.

Some bands of Native Americans harassed and attacked the Spanish camp numerous times over the next two weeks. On April 12, the British attacked the camp with their largest force yet, east of Bayou Chico. This assault proved to be a fruitless and wasteful exercise, and the British did not waste any more energy on the camp. General Gálvez was seriously wounded, however, and his command was transferred to José de Ezpeleta while he slowly recovered.

◄ Portrait of General Captain of the Armada Bote on the deck of a captured frigate. (Library of Congress)

On the morning after the failed assault, the vast majority of their Native American allies abandoned the British, nearly 400 in total. This brought their total garrison strength down to just 1,800 men. On the other side, over the following week reinforcements from Havana arrived—an additional 3,000 Spanish and 700 French soldiers. A joint Spanish-French fleet commanded by General Captain of the Armada Bote and Lieutenant General of the Navy François-Aymar de Monteil arrived in Pensacola Bay, and now the total Spanish army numbered upwards of 8,000. Unusually, for a battle against the British at that time, they also had naval superiority in the area.

The Siege of Pensacola

The British Royal Navy Redoubt, a five-faced battery made from earth and logs, attempted to counteract the Spanish fleet's movement. While the main British army gathered in Fort George to prepare for a siege, General Gálvez was hard at work moving men and artillery into place from the west. There were several modest British defensive lines, and the surprisingly hilly landscape of the region made the advance slow work. In addition, both sides had to pause briefly when another storm entered the area and halted the conflict.

The natural sounds of lightning and thunder soon gave way to the continuous roar of Spanish and British cannon fire. The majority of April had seen many small-scale skirmishes, but these only made way for larger-scale conflict. A particularly vicious clash was a fight for the hill and freshwater spring north of modern-day Attacks Court. For the Spanish it would mean a great place to begin siege works. It took four days, but the Spanish finally won the hill. The next day they began rotating 1,500 men in 12-hour shifts to dig siege

▶ The proud guns of Fort George in Pensacola. (Author's Collection)

▼ Spanish troops making landfall. (Florida State Archives)

The Spanish Army

As we begin the breakdown of the final major struggle for control of West Florida during the Revolutionary War, it's worth taking a closer look at the unusual army that faced the British in the campaign for West Florida.

Significantly, Spain had a most cosmopolitan group of soldiers to fight the British in Pensacola. The Spanish forces that landed on Santa Rosa Island included a large unit from Mallorca, a biracial group that had among its ranks many Afro-Cubans. It also had a Hibernian regiment of Irish soldiers which were led by Colonel Arturo O'Neill. For obvious reasons, many Irish Catholics had fled to Spain, and Colonel O'Neill (whose family had fled Ireland when he was 16) proved an adept leader of what was an important fighting force for Spain throughout the latter half of the 18th century and for several years beyond. The Spanish forces were also augmented by a number of Creole speakers and free Black people from Louisiana.

Colonel O'Neill's unit, which we must assume was particularly motivated to fight, was able to force the British off the island and into Pensacola Bay. At this point, most British forces were huddled in Fort George, which had been constructed in 1772 and prepared for a long siege. Captain de Irázabal claimed his mission was finished after pursuing the fleeing British into the bay, so he left with his fleet and sailed for Havana.

Colonel O'Neill's Irish contingent landed on the mainland on March 28 and faced a relentless attack from Britain's Native American allies, the Choctaws. Colonel O'Neill and General Gálvez's forces were augmented by additional troops arriving from Mobile—effectively the occupation force that had been left there earlier in the year.

The Gulf Coast Campaign

▶ Remains of the once mighty Fort George in Pensacola, Florida. (Author's Collection)

▼ The proud cannons of Fort King George still stand watch today. (Author's Collection)

works. On May 5, 1781, General Gálvez positioned a battery on a height within range of Fort George and opened fire. The British responded in kind, starting a chain of heavy exchanges.

The Spanish used infantry trenches and batteries to wear down British defenses. At one point the British answered by overrunning and destroying one of the batteries. Nevertheless, the siege continued at a sluggish pace with both sides failing to make much headway.

In the first week of May, it was already clear that the siege was not proceeding

The Florida Campaign, 1774–83

◀ Coehorn mortar at Fort George. (Author's Collection)

as expected. The French troops were grumbling about General Gálvez's leadership and had started threatening to leave if there wasn't a breakthrough. On May 6, the frustrated French announced that they would be withdrawing from the battle. General Gálvez, as ever, remained undaunted.

Importantly, this was a critical engagement for the French navy, which wanted to ensure that the British could not use Florida as a staging ground for attacks in the Caribbean. As we will soon discuss, French success in this battle directly impacted the course of the war and the cause of American independence.

As the siege continued, each night General Gálvez would move his cannons, probing the walls, looking for some breakthrough. Each day the citizens within would hold their breaths, hide in panic from possible debris, and hope that the Spanish wouldn't breach the walls. Their only hope was that somehow the defenders would wear down their enemies and save their city.

On the bright morning of May 8, a Spanish battery was moved to a portion of the fort it had hit earlier in the siege. General Gálvez had been staring at it. It looked promising. The Spanish battery aimed and fired, and a large part of the fort blew off. Stone and masonry scattered in the air and in every direction. Everyone was stunned, attacker and defender alike. The sound was deafening. The shot had

▼ A historical marker located at Fort George. (Author's Collection)

▲ Painting of General Gálvez in the center of the action at the siege of Pensacola, by Augusto Ferrer-Dalmau. (National Museum of U.S. Army)

▶ Sons of the American Revolution Florida Society Plaque. (Florida State Parks)

▲ The Siege of Pensacola. Here we see the "lucky shot" that exploded the Fort George's powder magazine. (Library of Congress)

◀ One-in-a-million shot. (Artist Kenny Maguire)

landed in the doorway of the fort's powder magazine and ignited the main supply of gunpowder.

According to historian David Head, the lucky shot took place while General Gálvez was in the middle of his morning routine of washing. He heard the explosion, saw the storm of carnage left in its wake, and knew the time had come. Turning to his men, many of whom were straining at the leash to race toward the fort, the governor gave the simple command to overwhelm them!

It was a one-in-a-million shot. At best, the Spanish must have hoped the shot would create an opening through which they could enter the fort. Instead, it killed nearly 100 men instantly, crippled the fort, destroyed its supplies, and effectively ended the entire siege. Once this happened, all Loyalists who were able to leave abandoned the city, and the British lost nearly all their Native American allies by the end of the day. It was over; West Florida had fallen. The defenders were now hopelessly outnumbered and had lost the will to fight. They knew General Gálvez was a gentleman, however, and that they would receive good terms, so Pensacola fell formally on May 10 when the British commander, Brigadier General Campbell, surrendered his 1,100 remaining troops.

Afterword

By the end of May 1781 the entirety of West Florida had fallen into Spanish hands. General Gálvez prepared at this time to attack Jamaica and potentially East Florida. Colonel O'Neill was appointed

▲ In the 1890s, tourists look over one of the blown-out openings from the Spanish siege. (Library of Congress)

◀ Statue erected in Pensacola in honor of the bicentennial of General Gálvez's birth. (Author's Collection)

The Florida Campaign, 1774–83

royal governor of West Florida. At this point, East Florida continued to be secure and a militarized protector of British possessions in the Caribbean, despite facing potential French and Spanish attacks during the final phase of the Revolutionary War.

The victory at Pensacola had a direct impact on the course of the war, and encouraged the French navy to repeat the effort by similarly bottling up the British escape routes at Yorktown later that year.

Even though the Continental Army was not present at Pensacola or in most of the battles that led to the fall of West Florida, the campaign was critical for the survival of the new United States. Moreover, the French fleet was not only successful at Pensacola in aiding the Spanish but was now free to help General Washington and his Patriot forces.

The French also learned the lesson that if they could bottle up the British land forces in tough terrain surrounded by water, despite the strength of the Royal Navy, victory was possible. Much like what would happen later in the year at Yorktown, the Royal Navy and British reinforcements were dispatched late to Pensacola and the battle was effectively lost long before British planners determined to change the course of proceedings.

Make no mistake. What had taken place was quite simply the greatest Spanish military victory of the war, and possibly of an entire age. It would have lasting consequences for both empires and would open the door to the eventual American purchase of Florida. Within a generation,

▲ Historical marker dedicated to the campaign. (Florida State Parks)

▶ General Gálvez's Florida campaign would immortalize him as a military hero. His statue stands proudly in Pensacola. (National Park Service)

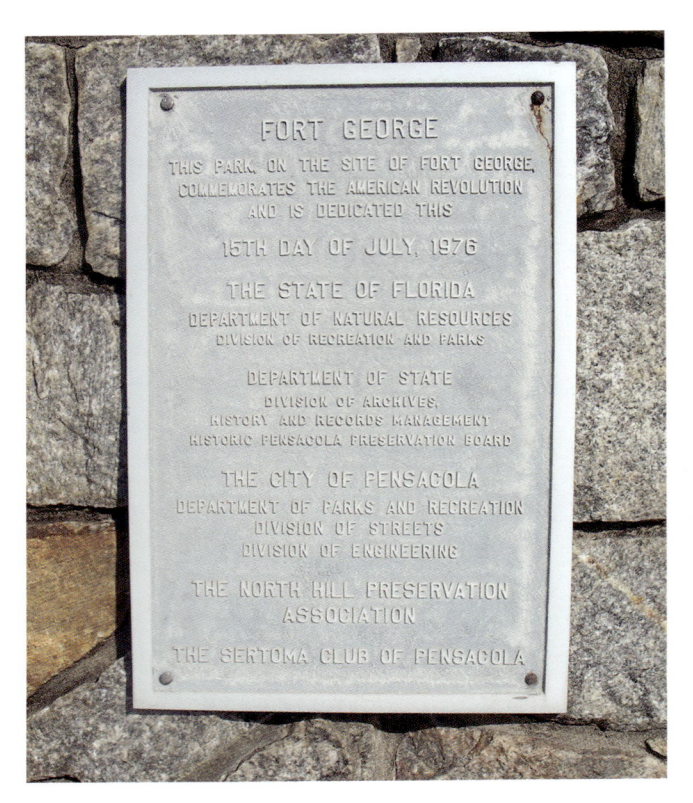

▲ Fort Matanzas during high tide. (Author's Collection)

all the great Spanish forts in Florida would be flying the Stars and Stripes. But for the present, Spain was victorious.

The successful siege of Pensacola and the conquest of West Florida was now complete. General Gálvez had aided the American cause in the most extraordinary of ways and had earned his nation back a good measure of its pride. There would be no meaningful British opposition in West Florida for the remainder of the war. For every remaining Loyalist in Florida, there was only one course left to them: evacuation.

A Fortress Territory

With the Revolution raging in Georgia and the Carolinas, East Florida became a fortress colony for Great Britain. It was not only needed as a refuge for Loyalists fleeing from the colonies but as a staging area for reinforcements and supplies, and as a base from which to protect British interests in the Caribbean. This became even more important once West Florida fell to the Spanish in May 1781, and the Americans and French were triumphant at Yorktown that November.

The governance and military operations around East Florida from late 1778 until 1783 indicated that Britain intended to make the colony a fortress which took in Loyalists from other colonies, and a beachhead from which to protect its important Caribbean holdings which were now threatened by both the French and Spanish.

▼ Fort Matanzas was built by the Spanish to guard the Matanzas inlet and for the indirect defense of St. Augustine. (National Park Service)

A Fortress Territory

▲ Convicts, slaves, and troops were used to construct Fort Menendez. Water was a constant scarcity for those undertaking the fort's construction. (Author's Collection)

Against this backdrop, East Florida becoming a fortress for Great Britain takes on a different meaning than simply looking at it as a last beachhead south of the St. Lawrence River in North America. In fact, the period from 1778 to 1783 witnessed the sort of economic and population boom that East Florida wouldn't see again until Henry Flagler's arrival more than a hundred years later.

The State of the War

As the war began to turn markedly in favor of the American Patriots, more British Loyalists started to evacuate to St. Augustine. The once great British city of Savannah, with its Roman-like gardens and squares, became deserted. South Carolina, including its proud jewel, Charleston, became emptied. The streets of St. Augustine were flooded with new faces, packed with families and their scattered possessions. They were turning to the last quiet corner of the region, trying to escape the war that had consumed so much of their lives. But as with all evacuations, tragedy seemed to follow.

By 1780, the American Revolution had become a world war. Battles raged in the Caribbean between the British and the French. The Spanish were advancing though West Florida, as we have described, And the Indian subcontinent saw battles between French proxies and the British East India Company. Even Europe itself wasn't immune from the conflict as naval battles raged in the Irish Sea and Bay of Biscay, while the Spanish eyed the "liberation" of Gibraltar.

▶ A modern look at Fort Menendez during its annual high tide when the surrounding area is flooded. (National Park Service)

▲ Photograph of Fort Matanzas. East Florida as a whole had become a large fortress. (Author's Collection)

The surrender of Cornwallis's army to General Washington's forces on October 19, 1781, prompted the British government to begin the negotiations which led to the end of the Revolutionary War. After the fall of Yorktown, decisive battles between the once mighty British army and the newly confident American forces gave way to peace talks, and little but small backwoods skirmishes for the remainder of the conflict in North America.

The British still occupied New York City when the Treaty of Paris was initially signed in November 1782, but Savannah and Charleston were either fully empty of British troops or in the process of being evacuated. North American port cities formerly under British control emptied their Loyalist inhabitants into the waters of the Atlantic, while the inland Loyalists clogged the back roads and trails near the borders of Canada and East Florida. Nova Scotia, Quebec, England, the Bahamas, the British West Indies, and Central America became ports of call for countless loyal emigrants. In every direction, people were trying to outrun the new and foreign concept of American Independence that had at long last triumphed over the Old World.

Worldwide, aside from the Thirteen Colonies, British forces had been suffering a demoralizing succession of losses at Minorca, Florida, and the West Indies. Just as the Seven Years' War had been the first major global conflict in human history, with battlefields spread across the continents, the Revolutionary War had delivered dramatic and costly consequences for all the major empires. In that earlier conflict England had been the victor, yet it was a victory won at a terrible financial cost that would result in the second global contest: the American Revolutionary War.

Now England had lost most of its North American holdings, and its naval power was under siege across the globe by Franco-

◂ St. Augustine's old Spanish houses. (Library of Congress)

A Fortress Territory

▶ Once a quiet backwater community, St. Augustine became flooded with refugees during the Revolutionary War. (Library of Congress)

Spanish forces. But the most important of Britain's New World possessions were in the Caribbean. It is difficult for modern readers to imagine, but places like Jamaica, Dominica, and Barbados were far more economically important to the mother country in the 1780s than its territories currently in the United States.

Simply put, Britain had to protect its Caribbean possessions. What had started out as a messy colonial war of minor consequence was now a global war in which the mighty British Empire was on its back foot. As a result, having essentially become an outsize fortress in and of itself, East Florida became a critical staging ground for the efforts of the Crown to hang on to the Caribbean.

Provincial Legislature of East Florida

The 1778 influx of Loyalists into East Florida finally changed the composition of the population to where Governor Tonyn

▶ The old City Gates of St. Augustine during the war. (Library of Congress)

The Florida Campaign, 1774–83

felt elections were possible. So, for the first time, East Florida gave the franchise to large landowners—with the assumption that they were sympathetic to the Crown and not to the Patriot cause. In late 1779, Governor Tonyn finally put forth plans for the provincial legislature in East Florida to be elected by popular ballot.

The election was held throughout the colony among landowners who possessed at least 500 acres. The first provincial assembly was seated in March 1781. The 19-man assembly was forced to raise taxes on the citizenry, as well as pledge allegiance to King George III, further separating East Florida from the Patriot cause. Florida had never had regular elections of any kind under Spanish rule, so this was a first for the colony.

Some of the 19 newly elected members sought to deal with the question of slavery by imposing a harsh slave code, foreshadowing what would happen when the Floridas became part of the United States in 1821.

However, Governor Tonyn's wish to continue arming African Americans factored into the assembly's compromise on the matter. Also of importance in the decision not to impose a harsh slave code was the growing abolitionist movement in the mother country. In addition, there was the very practical concern about identifying enslaved versus free African people, which led to inaction on the question.

Colonel John Leslie and Thomas Forbes, two Loyalist exiles from other Southern Colonies, were among those elected to the legislature.

East Florida as a Tory Safe Haven, 1781–83

Following the British defeat at Yorktown, Loyalists began flooding into East Florida. In 1782 alone, over 6,000 refugees arrived in the peninsula. The assumption in this period was that East Florida would remain part of the British Empire, even though West Florida had fallen out of British hands. This influx furthered the massive wave of Loyalists that had come in 1778.

While American history now records the surrender at Yorktown as decisive, British war planners in the winter of 1781/82 did not see Cornwallis's defeat as in any way conclusive. King George III was initially resolved to fight on, as the British still held New York City and East Florida at the time, as well as scoring successes in battle against the French in the Caribbean. The thought was that the battle fronts were shifting but the war itself was far from over.

During colonial times, St. Augustine's shallow inlet and sandbar made it a difficult target to reach by sea. This is part of what made the sieges of the city in 1702 and 1740 so remarkable, because it was

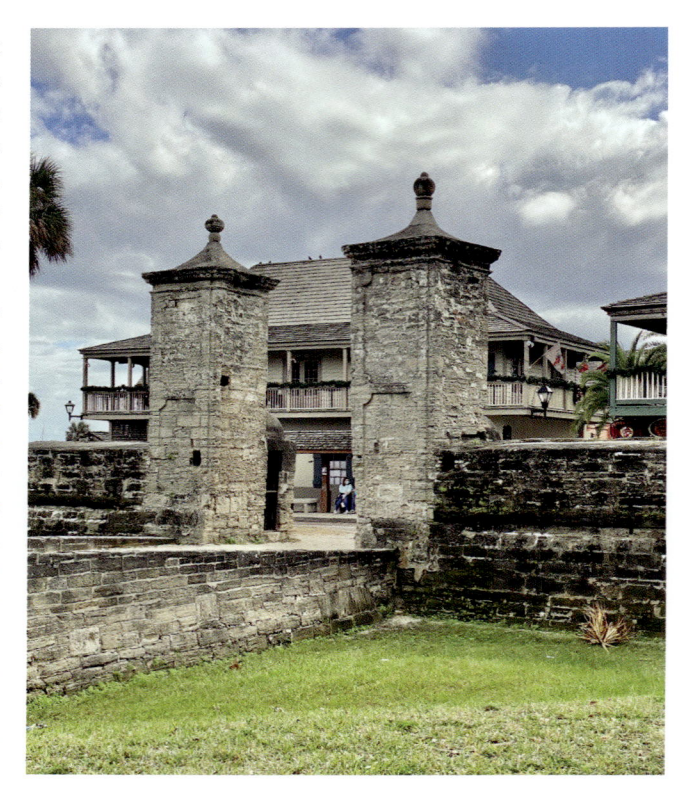

▲ St. Augustine's City Gates today. (Author's Collection)

A Fortress Territory

a locale largely immune from the use of massive sea power, something Britain had in abundance.

Even if the sandbar could be navigated, the channel into the Matanzas River was almost as treacherous and filled with potential danger. During the Revolutionary War this protected St. Augustine from American privateers as well as the French and Spanish navies that in the later stages of the conflict hovered in close proximity to the town.

Tory refugees flooded into East Florida as American independence seemed inevitable. This mass movement swelled the population in and around St. Augustine to 15,000 (five times what the population had been at the start of the conflict) or perhaps even more. This influx included many plantation owners bringing their enslaved with them, as well as free Black people who had run away behind British lines. British military officials also began pouring into St. Augustine at this juncture.

It is often not appreciated how much the Loyalists that fled the Carolinas and Georgia sacrificed in the way of property and comfort to escape to St. Augustine. Patriot control of the Southern Colonies absolutely terrified many Loyalists. Explaining this fear is difficult in hindsight given our prevailing views on republicanism and monarchy in the 21st century. Suffice to say that wartime clashes between Patriots and Loyalists had often been vicious in nature, and when the Patriots fully gained the upper hand, many Loyalists realized they needed to flee.

St. Augustine was a town that wasn't prepared for this influx—already swelling from Loyalist refugees and British troops during the course of the war, after Yorktown it became an untenable situation. In fact, East Florida, which was seen as a backwater at the start of the conflict, now suddenly had nearly as many people in and around its capital as Boston, New York, and Philadelphia.

The influx was a boon for merchants, as bakeries, taverns, butchers, vegetable stalls, and billiard parlors overflowed with new business. Hardware and clothing stores sprung up in the city. St. George's Street in particular was overflowing with business, and the plaza area near the Governor's House was teeming with activity and merchant stalls. St. Augustine had recovered the vibrancy it once had as a key part of Spain's colonial project in the 1600s.

The Spanish still harbored designs on East Florida, having recaptured West Florida, and in 1782, they defeated the British in the Bahamas. The conquest of the Bahamas brought fear to East Florida, and the nascent provincial legislature passed an act requiring all males between 15 and 60 to perform militia service.

▼ Map of St. Augustine in the 1770s, during the second Spanish period. (Library of Congress)

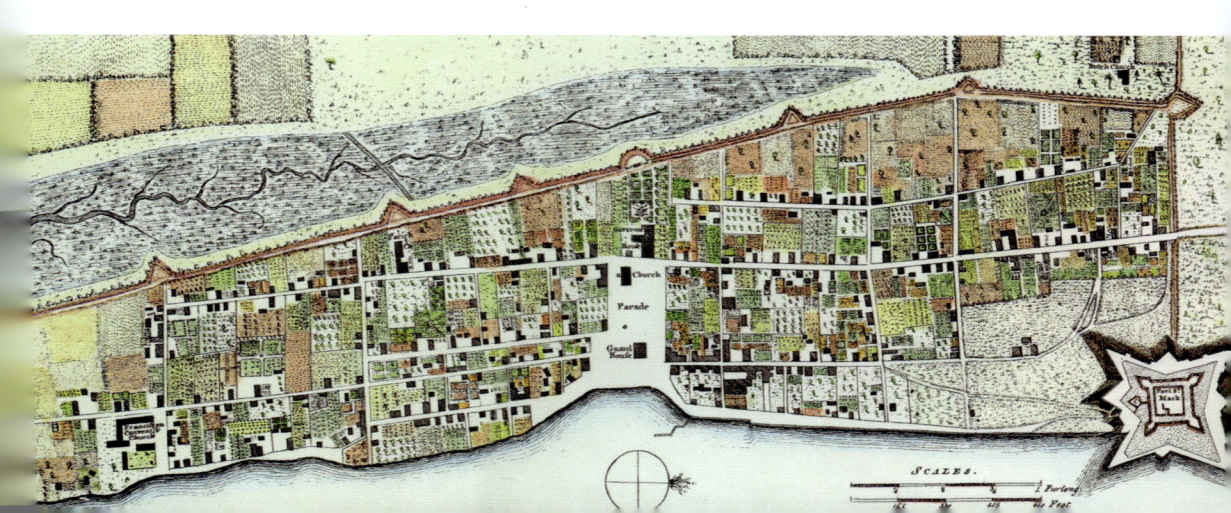

The Florida Campaign, 1774–83

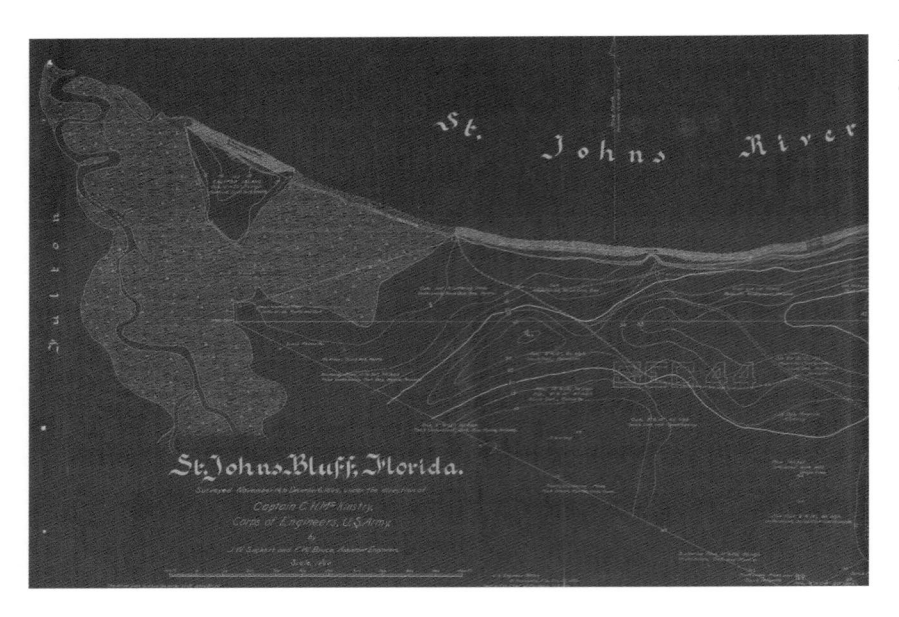

◀ St. Johns Bluff—a Tory safe haven. (Library of Congress)

Spain was also effective in raiding the outlying area of the Florida peninsula during this period, leading to detachments of soldiers being order by Governor Tonyn to protect Mosquito Inlet and the Halifax River, as well as St. Johns Bluff and the lower reaches of Anastasia Island.

An attack on East Florida seemed inevitable in 1782, as the Revolutionary War had shifted into a more global conflict with battles between the British and the Patriot-aligned European powers taking place all over the world.

However, the British were determined to keep East Florida, and Tories kept flowing into the colony. This flow of refugees not only included planters and their enslaved, as noted above, but also merchants, artisans, and farmers. Even though the noose was tightening over British control of East Florida, a hope persisted, perhaps naively, that St. Augustine and its surrounding areas would remain tied to the kingdom of King George III.

◀ Slowly, strategic forts across the region were emptied. Shown here is a small British fortification built on the St. Johns River. (Library of Congress)

St. Johns Bluff and its Loyalists

With the influx of Loyalists fleeing colonies to the North, a new settlement, roughly where the reconstructed Fort Caroline and the Timucuan National Preserve lies today, was founded during the war. The town was on the south bank of the St. Johns River about five miles from the Atlantic seashore.

In June 1782, this area was designated an area for refugees to be resettled. By the end of that year, 6,000 people had been transported from St. Augustine to the settlement, which previously only had a few hundred residents. The proprietor of this area, Thomas Williamson, had been granted 200 acres in 1779, and he divided the land accordingly to help resettle the influx of Loyalists from the colonies.

During the period between June 1782 and the middle of 1783, hundreds of new homes were built, as were facilities on the waterfront. These new structures facilitated commerce, and the springing up virtually overnight of a merchant and trade-based economy.

About 300 houses were constructed in the town and Governor Tonyn was encouraged that St. Johns Bluff on the navigable St. Johns River could become a great merchant hub and seaport in the future. Blacksmiths, bakers, and shipbuilders were relocated from St. Augustine, and the town developed a vibrancy to make it East Florida's "second city" by the middle of 1783.

Following the return of East Florida to Spain in 1784, however, the town was dismantled, and since the vast majority of Loyalists were unwilling to live under Spanish rule, little trace of it exists today.

Still, the short-lived community of St. Johns Bluff can be considered the inspiration for Jacksonville, which sprang up in a similar geographic area decades later, and today is Florida's largest city.

The British had a strict policy to leave areas west of the St. Johns River to the natives, meaning new white settlers fleeing

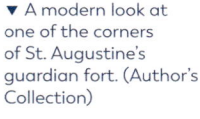

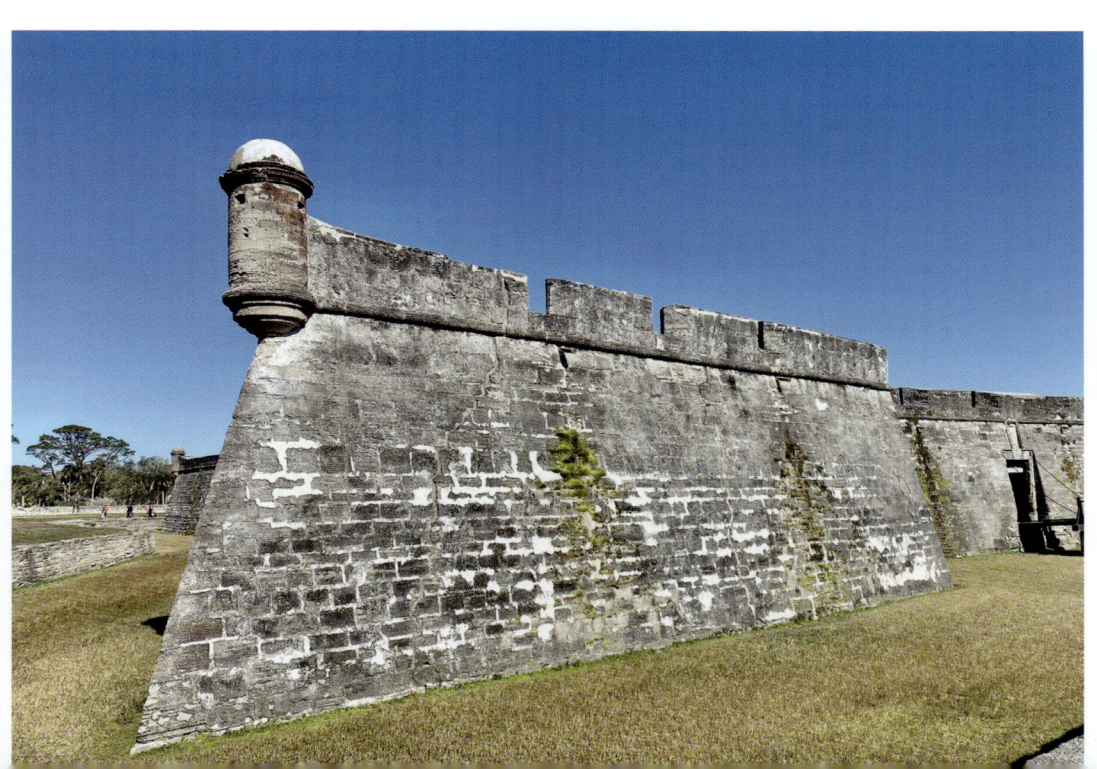

▼ A modern look at one of the corners of St. Augustine's guardian fort. (Author's Collection)

the Patriot army to the north had to remain east of the St. Johns, south of the next town.

Military Developments in 1782

Brigadier General Archibald McArthur was placed in command of the British Southern District based in St. Augustine. As Loyalists continued to flow into the colony, concerns continued to be raised that St. Augustine could be attacked from the sea. This fear intensified after the fall of Nassau in the Bahamas to the Spanish in the middle of 1782.

During the year, more Native Americans, largely from the Creek tribe, came to Florida, fleeing to British territory with the assumed coming cession of the areas west of the Appalachians to the new United States.

The arrival of more natives, while welcomed by British authorities, was resented by many Loyalists, as supplies and resources were in increasingly short supply as the population of the colony swelled.

Loyalist Shipwrecks

Unfortunately, the stories of mass refugees seeking to remain under British rule in East Florida are not as pleasant or straightforward as we'd like.

There is ambiguity about the number of ships that ran aground trying to navigate the tricky entrance to St. Augustine harbor, but many resulted in the loss of property, and in some cases lives. One thing we can

▲ The interior of Fort St. Mark. Once the French and Spanish came into the war, the British worried that St. Augustine could be attacked from the sea. (Library of Congress)

◄ St. Augustine harbor. (Library of Congress)

ascertain for certain is that over 25 ships had accidents, and dozens of lives, perhaps more, were certainly lost.

One particular set of shipwrecks has caught the imagination of generations—the New Year's shipwrecks of 1782/83.

In mid-December 1782, 16 ships filled with Loyalists, soldiers, and cargo left Charleston bound for St. Augustine. These ships were just the latest of hundreds that made the journey from Charleston or Savannah to St. Augustine in 1782 carrying Loyalists and British military.

The ships, like so many before, had trouble navigating the sandbar and the channel. To complicate matters, a violent winter storm ravaged the area.

In the end, none of the 16 ships made it to harbor. The loss of life was substantial (we don't have exact numbers), though many of the passengers were rescued or made it to Anastasia Island. However, all the cargo was lost.

Some of the recovered or salvaged cargo can be seen at various sites in Florida, including the St. Augustine Lighthouse and Museum and the Mel Fisher Treasure Museum in Sebastian.

The *East Florida Gazette*

East Florida, as a sparsely populated, seemingly far-flung population, never had its own local newspaper—until 1782.

Because most of the news that made its way to St. Augustine had long been brought via newspapers from Savannah or Charleston, Patriot sentiments were often circulated among those who read newspapers in the East Florida capital. But the influx of Loyalists from other colonies, which made St. Augustine one of the most populated places in North America by 1782, meant a local newspaper was badly needed.

Dr. William Charles Wells, a Charleston Loyalist who fled the South Carolina capital in 1782, brought his printing press with him to St. Augustine and began printing the *East Florida Gazette* in January 1783. The paper was published until April 1784, and featured news from a Loyalist perspective.

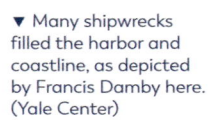

▼ Many shipwrecks filled the harbor and coastline, as depicted by Francis Damby here. (Yale Center)

The Florida Campaign, 1774–83

One of the most famous editions of the *Gazette* was published in April 1783 when the British under the direction of St. Augustine-based Loyalist Colonel Deveaux liberated the Bahamas from Spanish occupation. Ironically, many of the paper's readers would end up relocating to the Bahamas within 18 months.

At the start of the war there were approximately 4,000 non-natives in East Florida. By April 20, 1783, there were 21,735 recorded people in the colony of either European or African blood. So we can surmise there were 17,500 or more refugees.

The Liberation of the Bahamas—an East Florida Operation

As noted above, Colonel Deveaux led an operation to liberate the Bahamas from Spanish control. He recruited a total of about 150 men, both white and Black, to undertake the mission.

> ### Where Did the East Florida Loyalists Go?
>
> Of the Loyalists forced to leave East Florida in 1783–84, about 3,500 went to the Bahamas, 1,000 went to Jamaica, approximately 800 went to Nova Scotia, around 650 went to other parts of the British Caribbean, and 300 even resettled in Britain itself. It is likely the bulk of those 3,500 or so not accounted for either migrated farther west to today's Alabama and Mississippi or may have settled in other parts of the British Empire including what is now Ontario.

The volunteers gathered in St. Augustine in mid-March 1783, and left the city on April 1. After landing on New Providence and engaging in a few minor battles, the force liberated Nassau on April 18. However, the Spanish had already agreed

▼ Troops attempting to take over the Bahamas. (Library of Congress)

A Fortress Territory

to cede the Bahamas to Britain on April 9 during peace negotiations in Europe. This was completely unknown to the fighters since news traveled across the Atlantic very slowly in 1783.

The Last Naval Battle of the War

The final naval battle between British and Patriot forces took place off the Florida coast in March 1783. Financier Robert Morris had arranged a shipload of Spanish gold and silver to be taken from Havana to Philadelphia. Captain John Barry sailed in the USS *Alliance* from Martinique to Havana, and then onward to Newport, Rhode Island, accompanied by the USS

◄ Portrait of Colonel Andrew Deveaux, Loyalist soldier and later hero of the British Bahamas. (Library of Congress)

▼ Florida was the site of one of the last naval battles of the war. This artwork shows the USS *Alliance*, USS *Duc de Lauzun*, HMS *Alarm*, HMS *Sybil*, and HMS *Tobago* engaged in action. (U.S. Naval Academy Museum)

Duc De Lauzun, commanded by Captain John Green.

The HMS *Sybil*, commanded by Captain Vashon, the HMS *Alarm*, and the HMS *Tobago* engaged in battle against the American ships about 140 miles southeast of Cape Canaveral.

After a fierce shelling from both sides, which lasted 45 minutes (and included a sixth ship, the French frigate *Triton*), the battle ended with an American victory and about 40 dead on the *Sybil*, which, along with its British companion boats, sailed off in defeat.

The American and French ships pursued the fleeing British fleet, but to no avail. The American ships then sailed to their destination.

▲ The Continental Navy fiercely battles the Royal Navy near Cape Canaveral. (U.S. Naval Academy Museum)

◄ Captain James Vashon leads his men as they prepare to board a British vessel. (Library of Congress)

A Fortress Territory

The battle, which took place about 100 miles east of present-day Cocoa Beach, was among the last military engagements of the conflict, and was the very last naval battle fought between American and British forces until the War of 1812.

This relatively small engagement also served as a reminder of the hundreds of encounters at sea against the British that were not decisive but, coupled with the constant threats and periodic setbacks on land, chipped away at the logistics, the morale, and ultimately the will of that powerful nation. It also helped establish gallant traditions that would help shape what would later become the most powerful navy in the history of the world.

◀ Portrait of Captain (later commodore) John Barry, U.S. Navy, commanding officer of the last naval battle of the Revolutionary War. Portrait by Gilbert Stuart. (U.S. Naval Historical Center)

▼ The brief battle off Cape Canaveral became an important chapter in Florida history. (Library of Congress)

The Florida Campaign, 1774–83

Treaty of Paris, 1783

The war between the United States and Great Britain was formally ended by the Treaty of Paris in September 1783. This treaty confirmed American independence. However, Florida was not included in Britain's territorial concession to the United States. While this wasn't a major point of contention at the time with the American delegation, it soon would be, as Florida became an object of the newly independent nation's desire. However, the United States, under its lead negotiator, Chief Justice of the U.S. Supreme Court John Jay, was already growing wary of the Spanish during the negotiations, a factor that would set up the coming conflicts between the two nations.

Treaty of Versailles, 1783

On the same day as the Treaty of Paris, the adjoining Treaty of Versailles ended hostilities between Britain on one side, and France, Spain, and the Dutch Republic on the other. In this treaty, East Florida was formally ceded to Spain, and West Florida was confirmed as a Spanish territory. It was not a foregone conclusion that Britain would cede East Florida, but the potentially heavy expense of defending an isolated colony led to Britain handing it to Spain. There was some controversy among the British diplomats, who claimed that in ceding West Florida, the British were giving the Spanish more territory than they had received from them in 1763. This was because of the areas formerly part of French Louisiana that had been attached to West Florida.

▲ The frigate USS *Alliance* was the last ship remaining in the Continental Navy. (Library of Congress)

▲▶ Historical marker for the battle. (Author's Collection)

▶ A cannon from the naval battle. (Author's Collection)

A Fortress Territory

Ultimately, the British did think that ceding both Floridas to Spain was preferable to ceding them to the new United States.

However, while the Treaty of Paris had clearly specified the St. Marys River as the boundary between the new United States and East Florida, the territory as well as the navigational rights on the rivers of West Florida (except the Apalachicola) were not clearly defined by either treaty and would lead to a decade-long border dispute between Spain and the United States.

A takeaway from this treaty that would impact world history was that Britain keeping its Caribbean holdings meant that France's gamble to join the American Revolution had probably failed. The only way France could justify the expenditure of helping the Patriots was to capture some of the resource-rich islands of the British Caribbean. The failure to capture these islands contributed directly to the discontent which set up the French Revolution.

Evacuation of the Colony

East Florida's status as a fortress colony in the South made it unique in the British North American landscape. While the top British military brass, including Commander in Chief Guy Carleton, felt that evacuating East Florida and marshalling resources in the Caribbean was strategically wise after Yorktown, they resisted issuing proclamations to that effect because of a feeling that Loyalists fleeing the other Southern Colonies needed a place of refuge.

▲ The Treaty of Paris. (Library of Congress)

◀ 1783's Treaty of Versailles was met with great celebration. (Library of Paris)

▲ East Florida was the chief site of Tory evacuations back to England. (Library of Congress)

Despite this, the British treaty negotiators and military leadership saw East Florida as isolated, and a piece to give up as a bargaining chip when dealing with Spain, France, and the United States.

By the middle of 1783 it was obvious based on developments elsewhere that East Florida would be ceded either to Spain or the United States, though the former seemed more likely. This was confirmed by the Treaty of Versailles on September 3, 1783. Governor Tonyn, for his part, knew this cession to Spain was coming from about April of 1783 onward, and began readying the colonial authorities for an eventual evacuation.

Despite Governor Tonyn's intentions, and Spain giving Britain an 18-month transition period, a rather hasty evacuation of the colony took place in 1784. The orders issued in London on December 4, 1783, reached Governor Tonyn in early 1784. On May 6, Governor Tonyn issued an order to undertake an orderly evacuation, and asked all East Florida residents looking to leave the colony to contact the authorities by the end of May. Transport would be provided at the public expense.

▼ Eventually the British departed the New World for the Old. (U.S. Naval Academy Museum)

A Fortress Territory

General Washington reclaiming New York. (Library of Congress)

But many if not most of the colony's residents were not happy with this. Those who had fled the other Southern Colonies were just settling down to life in East Florida and did not want to move again. Native Americans, having felt their treatment more just by the British than the Spanish or the colonists to the north, foraged through the shops of St. Augustine. Bandits led by the infamous Lieutenant Colonel McGirt raided plantations throughout the St. Johns River area.

Lieutenant Colonel Brown and his Rangers of all races generally moved to Nova Scotia. Many of the wealthier Loyalists headed for the Caribbean, most notably the Bahamas, Jamaica, and Dominica. Some evacuees ended up in the British Isles themselves, but this was probably no more than a few hundred of the 19,000 that evacuated East Florida.

The evacuation was not only hasty but brought a certain lawlessness to the colony, something that would continue under Spanish rule.

One resident who did not evacuate was Lieutenant Colonel McGirt, whose activities caught the notice of Spanish authorities, who put him and his bandits on trial. Found guilty, McGirt was hauled away to Havana to serve a five-year sentence. Eventually Lieutenant Colonel McGirt escaped and returned to his Patriot roots, and lived out his days in Charleston.

When the evacuation was complete in late 1784, all but about 2,000 of East Florida's 21,000 residents had left the colony. Meanwhile, in West Florida, the colony's population, which had not swelled during the Revolution, and had now been effectively governed by Spain since 1779 or 1781, remained in place.

Those who moved to the Bahamas, particularly the island of New Providence, were given generous land grants. The liberation of the islands had come under the direction of Brigadier General McArthur, who had been based in St. Augustine at the time.

Conclusion

As discussed in the Fortress Colony section, the Treaty of Versailles formally ceded East and West Florida to Spain. The British government agreed to pay Floridians for their lost property, but this didn't satisfy most of them, so they were offered valuable land in the Bahamas. This did the trick, and most of the settlers accepted the arrangement and abandoned the colony of Florida. After just 21 tumultuous years, the British flag was lowered, and Florida once again became part of a rejuvenated Spanish empire.

When many Americans imagine scenes from the Revolutionary War, their mind's eye always turns toward colonial Virginia, Liberty Hall, or the harbor of Boston. But you need only to scratch the surface to find a mountain of sights throughout the South that played a role in America earning its independence. Nearly every location featured in this book is today a National Historical Park or landmark, or commemorated with monuments. Since the American Bicentennial, there has been an active reappraisal of British Florida and the Gulf Coast campaign.

This reappraisal has intensified since the emphasis on Governor Dunmore's proclamation on the role of African Americans, and the fate of the enslaved, and has become a more mainstream talking point in the United States. Additionally, in Britain the role the Floridas played in the conflict and the Crown's thinking has been

▼ A cannon overlooks Pensacola today. (National Park Service)

▲ An aerial view of Castillo de San Marcos. (Library of Congress)

▼ The cannons of St. Augustine. (National Park Service)

widely discussed in the historical literature. While American texts still often exclude discussions of the Florida campaigns, Andrew Roberts' recent biography of King George III mentions Florida two dozen times, as it was a central area of British war planning and diplomatic effort.

Today's writings about the American Revolution create a context and contain an analysis that wasn't always present before the American Bicentennial. As a result, more and more emphasis is being placed on the role of the South in general and on Florida specifically in analyses of the war.

As for the story of Florida, the war was by no means a closing chapter on its colonial period.

The return of the two Floridas to Spanish rule did not end British influence. European politics, in which Britain and Spain found themselves allies, as well as the desire for Britain to continue to cultivate and arm Native American allies against growing threats from the United States, meant Britain continued to have a hand in Florida's affairs for the next 35 years.

Despite their wartime alliance, relations soon turned frosty between the United States and Spain due to border disputes, where Spain inherited Britain's position as the ruler of the Floridas.

Less than a year after the treaties that ended the war, Spain closed the port of New Orleans to American goods. This devastated commerce, particularly for the Southern states. At the time, access to the deep interior of the lower South was only possible through two river systems—the Mississippi and the Apalachicola. The seaward entry to both at this point was in Spanish territory.

▲ The streets of St. Augustine still reveal both Spanish and English influences. (Author's Collection)

▼ National Park visitor centers keep these important sites alive. (National Park Service)

Conclusion

▲ A modern view of Fort Matanzas, which is available for visitors. (National Park Service)

By 1785, Spain had made agreements with each of the Native American tribes in West Florida to align with the Spanish. This would set the stage for Florida's next chapter.

Unlike the British, who had ruled East Florida with a firm hand, a degree of lawless anarchy accompanied restoration of Spanish rule in the colony. This would lead to an increase in runaway slaves to the colony as well as militant activity by Native Americans, often overtly encouraged by British authorities in the coming years.

European colonialism in this part of the New World would continue for some time. A number of Spaniards returned from their exiles in the Caribbean and renewed their attempts at developing Florida. But the damage was done, there was a new presence on their northern border, and the land was too large for them to control. Some settlers were already talking about independence from Spain or annexation by the United States. America had developed a passion and an appetite for pushing farther west, and the Spanish knew it was only a matter of time before Florida would come into their sights.

In the first decade of the 1800s America would inch closer and closer to annexation. Eventually Spain would bow to the pressure and exchange possession of Florida for millions of dollars in American currency. All of these subsequent events in Florida's history have their origins during the American Revolution—the important and monumental prelude to what would eventually become a massive reversal of power from the Old World to the New.

125

Further Reading

Over the last few years there has been increased interest in the historical narrative of the state of Florida, and in particular the events of the Revolutionary War. In addition to our own research on the ground in Florida, the following sources were consulted and serve as recommended additional reading on this time period and the Florida fronts.

Bunn, Mike. *Fourteenth Colony: The Forgotten Story of the Gulf South During America's Revolutionary Era*. Athens, GA: University of Georgia Press, 2020.

De Quesada, Alejandro M. *A History of Florida Forts: Florida's Lonely Outposts*. Charleston, SC: History Press, 2006.

Gannon, Michael, ed. *The History of Florida*. Gainesville, FL: University Press of Florida, 2018.

Gannon, Michael. *Florida: A Short History*. Gainesville, FL: University Press of Florida, 2003.

Head, David. *A Republic of Scoundrels: The Schemers, Intriguers, and Adventurers Who Created a New American Nation*. New York City, NY: Pegasus Books, 2023.

Horne, Gerald. *The Counter-Revolution of 1776: Slave Resistance and the Origins of the United States of America*. New York City, NY: NYU Press, 2014.

Kokomoor, Kevin. *La Florida: Catholics, Conquistadores, and Other American Origin Stories*. West Palm Beach, FL: Pineapple Press, 2023.

Leckie, Robert. *A Few Acres of Snow: The Saga of the French and Indian Wars*. Jossey Bass, Hoboken, NJ: Wiley, 1999.

Raah, James W. *Spain, Britain and the American Revolution in Florida*. Jefferson, NC: McFarland & Co., 2007.

Tebaux, Charlton. *A History of Florida*. Coral Gables, FL: University of Miami Press, 1980.

Wright, Jr, J. Leitch. *Florida in the American Revolution*. Gainesville, FL: University Press of Florida, 1989.

In addition, the following documentary series from PBS covers this period of Florida history and was viewed in advance of writing this text: PBS Documentary Series: "Secrets of Spanish Florida" (2017). The authors also recommend the artwork of Kenny Maguire and his accomplished catalog that effortlessly capture the look and feel of both American and Floridian history. Anyone interested in the images featured throughout this book should explore the mountains of photos, artwork, and documents within the National Portrait Gallery collection, the Florida State Archives, and the Library of Congress.

Lastly the authors encourage all readers to explore the various National Parks and historic sites featured throughout this book. These sites all tell the story of the monumental events that helped define the American Revolution and our national identity.

Index

Ahaya the Cowkeeper, Chief, 55–56
Alligator Creek Bridge, battle of, 7, 46–48
Altamaha River, 31, 46
Amelia Island, 41–42, 48
Anastasia Island, 19, 66, 110
Arnold, Benedict, 34

Bahamas, 106, 109, 112, 114–15, 121, 122
Baker, John, 38, 41, 43
Barry, John, 115, 117
Baton Rouge, 15, 71, 81–84
Betsy incident, 66
Boston, 17, 52–53, 109, 122
Brown, Thomas, 37–38, 41, 43, 45–47, 56, 77, 121
Bryan, Jonathan, 35

Cameron, Alexander, 77
Campbell, John, 74, 76–77, 80–81, 90, 101
Cape Canaveral, naval battle off, 115–17
Carleton, Guy, 119
Castillo de San Marcos, 7, 29, 53, 57, 63–66, 69, 123. *See also* Fort St. Mark
Charles III, King of Spain, 74–75
Charleston, 7, 16, 40, 55, 67, 69, 105–6, 113, 121
Clinton, Henry, 63, 74
Continental Army, 9, 28–29, 32, 34–35, 40, 43, 47, 65, 74, 89, 102
Continental Congress, 9, 28–29, 31, 37, 48, 75, 78
Cooper River, 69
Cornwallis, Charles, 51, 106, 108
Culpher Spy Ring, 49
Cumberland Sound, 45

Declaration of Independence, 61, 67
Deveaux, Andrew, 114–15
Dickinson, Alexander, 81
Drayton, William, 57
Dunmore, Gov. John Murray, 53, 58, 61–62, 122
Durnford, Elias, 85–87

East Florida Gazette, 113–14
East Florida Rangers, 17, 37–38, 41–43, 45, 46–48, 50, 121
East Florida
    first American invasion of, 7, 31–35
    second American invasion of, 7, 35–43
    third American invasion of, 7, 43–49
Elbert, Samuel, 38, 41–43, 45
Ezpeleta y Galdeano, José, 91, 95

Forbes, John, 67
Forbes, Thomas, 108
Fort Bute, 74, 79, 81–83
Fort Charlotte, 13, 84–87, 89, 91
Fort George, 6, 72, 88, 90, 95–98, 100
Fort Howe (formerly Fort Barrington), 45
Fort King George, 29–35, 97
Fort Matanzas, 7, 9, 65–66, 103, 104, 106, 125
Fort McIntosh, 35
Fort Menendez, 105
Fort New Richmond, 83
Fort St. Mark (formerly Castillo de San Marcos), 53, 59–60, 64–65, 67, 112

Gadsden, Christopher, 69
Gage, Thomas, 28, 52–53
Gálvez, Bernardo de, 13, 76–77, 79–87, 89, 91–93, 95–99, 101–3
George III, King of Great Britain and Ireland, 54, 58, 72, 108, 110, 123
Georgia militia, 34–35, 45
Georgia State Assembly, 43
Georgia, Whig takeover of, 7, 28, 37
Germain, George, 73
German/Hessian troops/mercenaries, 61, 64, 73, 82, 90
Greene, Nathanael, 51
Gwinnett, Button, 37–38

Havana, 15, 59, 76, 80, 85–86, 91, 95, 96, 115, 121
HMS *Hinchinbrooke*, 45
HMS *Lord Sandwich*, 69

HMS *Rebecca*, 42–43, 45
Hopothle Mico (Talassee King of the Creeks), 89–90
Houstoun, John, 45, 48
Howe, Robert, 34–35, 43, 45, 46, 48

Irázabal, José Calvo de, 91–92, 96

Kings Road, 34–35, 46
Kirkland, Moses, 56

Lake Pontchartrain, battle of, 82–83
Lee, Charles, 32–34, 45
Leslie, John, 108
Loyalists, 7, 9, 17, 28–29, 37, 42, 45, 51, 54, 59, 90–91, 103,107, 109, 111–13, 115
  refugees, 7, 9, 29, 37, 54, 56–57, 101, 103, 104–9, 111–14, 119, 121

McGirt, Daniel (aka McGirth, McGirtt), 50–51, 121
Mississippi River, 15, 72, 74, 76, 78–81, 83–85, 114, 124
Mobile, 13, 15, 71–72, 81, 84–87, 91, 96
Montgomery, Richard, 34
Morris, Robert, 79, 82, 115
Mowbray, John, 42

Nassau (Bahamas), 112, 114
Natchez, 15, 71, 79, 81, 84. *See also* Fort Panmure
Native Americans, 9, 17, 22, 27, 29, 37, 38, 41, 43, 50, 54–55, 57–58, 62–64, 66, 76–77, 81, 89, 91, 95, 96, 101, 112, 121, 124–25
  Cherokee, 54
  Choctaws, 76–77, 91, 96
  Creeks, 43, 54–55, 76, 89, 91, 112
  Seminoles, 43, 55, 57–58
New Orleans, 76, 80–82, 84, 91, 93, 124
New Smyrna Colony, 6, 29, 31, 55, 58
New York, 22, 33–34, 50, 59, 106, 108–9, 121

O'Neill, Arturo, 96, 101

Panis, Jacinto, 79–80
Patriots, 7, 8–9, 17, 21, 28–29, 31, 33, 35, 37–38, 42–43, 45–46, 48, 50–51, 52–55, 57–58, 60–62, 65, 67, 69, 70, 75, 79, 83, 102, 105, 108–10, 112–13, 115, 119, 121
Peña-Peck House (aka Dr. Peck's House), 39–41
Pensacola, 6, 7, 15, 63, 71–74, 77, 80–82, 84–88, 88–91, 93, 95, 96–97, 99, 100, 101–3, 122

Pickles, William, 82
Prevost, Alexander, 40, 46, 50–51, 59–61, 64
Rochambeau, Jean-Baptiste, 49, 51
Royal Navy, 15, 61, 66–67, 79, 82, 95, 102, 116
Rutledge, John, 31, 53, 67

Savannah, 28, 31, 34, 43, 45, 48–50, 53, 74, 105–6, 113
Screven, James, 46, 48, 50
Seven Years' War, 6, 14, 15, 74, 75, 82, 106
Skinner, Alexander, 55
slaves, 27, 29, 59, 61, 63, 81, 105, 125
Sons of Liberty, 37, 55, 57
St. Augustine, 6–7, 9, 15, 16, 17, 19, 21, 23, 25, 27–29, 31–32, 35, 38, 40–41, 43, 48–49, 51, 52–61, 63–67, 69, 71, 73–74, 82, 88, 104–14, 121, 123, 124
St. Johns Bluff, 45, 110, 111
St. Johns River, 34, 41–43, 45, 48, 55, 59, 64, 111, 121
St. Marys River, 23, 27, 41–43, 45–46, 50, 56, 119
Stamp Act (1765), 21

Thomas Creek, battle of, 7, 41–43, 47, 48
Tonyn, Patrick, 7, 9, 12, 17, 37–40, 43, 45–46, 51–60, 62–64, 69, 107–8, 110–11, 120
Treaty of Paris
  1763, 15, 82
  1782, 106
  1783, 118–19
Treaty of Versailles, 1783, 118–20, 122

Unzaga, Luis de, 76
USS *Alliance*, 115, 118
USS *Morris*, 82

Washington, George, 28, 32–35, 45, 48–49, 51, 65, 89, 102, 106, 121
Wells, William Charles, 113
West Florida, battle of, 70–87
Williamson, Andrew, 48
Williamson, Thomas, 111
Willing, James, 77–79
  raids, 77–79

Yorktown, British surrender at, 7, 102, 104, 106, 108–9, 119